[Ch. 1]
- Transition to ownership? 4
- Meaning of farming?
- Farmer vs Farm laborer
- white ag. communities losing youth —
  white migration off farm,
  creates oppy for immigrants
- orgs - help new farmers
  access land + resources.
- marketing models: cooperative
  marketing collective. 22
- POC farmers - 25
  Disadvantaged.
- Schism - b/w immigrant farmer, 25
  state, org orgs
- agrarian class hierarchy - 30

ch. 2 –
Discriminatory policies + day-today racism.
– Myth of Agricultural ladder 32

Food, Health, and the Environment

Series Editor: Robert Gottlieb, Henry R. Luce Professor of Urban and Environmental Policy, Occidental College

For a complete list of books published in this series, please see the back of the book.

The New American Farmer

Immigration, Race, and the Struggle for Sustainability

Laura-Anne Minkoff-Zern

The MIT Press
Cambridge, Massachusetts
London, England

© 2019 Massachusetts Institute of Technology

This book was set in ITC Stone Serif Std and ITC Stone Sans Std by Toppan Best-set Premedia Limite. Printed and bound in the United States of America.

Library of Congress Cataloging-in-Publication Data is available.

ISBN: 978-0-262-53783-4

10 9 8 7 6 5 4 3 2 1

In loving memory of my mother, Rosemary Minkoff, whose unconditional love and support continues to serve as the foundation of my accomplishments.

Contents

Series Foreword

The New American Farmer: Immigration, Race, and the Struggle for Sustainability is the seventeenth book in the Food, Health, and the Environment series. The series explores the global and local dimensions of food systems, and the issues of access, social, environmental, and food justice, and community well-being. Books in the series focus on how and where food is grown, manufactured, distributed, sold, and consumed. They address questions of power and control, social movements and organizing strategies, and the health, environmental, social, and economic factors embedded in food system choices and outcomes. As this book demonstrates, the focus is not only on food security and well-being but also on economic, political, and cultural factors as well as regional, state, national, and international policy decisions. Food, Health, and the Environment books therefore provide a window into the public debates, alternative and existing discourses, and multidisciplinary perspectives that have made food systems and their connections to health and the environment critically important subjects of study, and for social and policy change.

Robert Gottlieb, Occidental College
Series Editor (gottlieb@oxy.edu)

Acknowledgments

This book would not exist without the enduring and impressive stories of the farmers highlighted here. Their courage to pursue their dreams and generosity in sharing their insights has allowed me to create an archive of their experiences. It was with deep sadness that I made the decision to keep their names and faces anonymous (with the exception of those identified in photographs), given the political moment of publication. The farmers whose voices are heard in this book deserve recognition for their incredible accomplishments, and I will work for a future where no one needs to fear making their name public in this country. I can only hope my retelling of their stories can act as a guide, informing the general public as well as food and farming institutions, organizations, and media, to increase resources for and acknowledgment of this incredible group of farmers across the nation.

In each location where I did fieldwork, I was welcomed and guided by people who connected me to farmers and their allies. In California, where my research journey began, I am immensely grateful to Adam Sanders. He was my first introduction to the indigenous farmworker and farmer community, and over the past eight years, has created more connections for me than I can recount. He and his wife, Phoebe, continued to host me after I had moved to the East Coast, and sustained our conversations and work on issues of food and farm labor justice together. I am also grateful to the generosity and openness of staff and farmers at the Agriculture and Land-Based Training Association in Salinas, California, where I spent many hours sitting in on trainings and conducting interviews over the years.

In Washington, DC, Larry Laverentz, formally of the Refugee Agricultural Partnership Program in the Office of Refugee Resettlement, and Poppy Davis, formally at the US Department of Agriculture (USDA), both helped me grasp the national landscape for immigrants and refugees in agriculture. Michelle Dudley and Christine Balch at the Crossroads Community Food Network, Stephanie Romelczyk at Westmoreland County Extension, Debbie Bullock and Lucee Kossler at the Natural Resources Conservation Service, and Sherina Logan at the Farm Service Agency (FSA) all opened pathways for meeting farmers and understanding the DC-area producers coming from Virginia.

In New York, Chris Wayne of Grow NYC and the FARMroots program, Marie Ullrich of Cooperative Extension, and Ford Barber from the FSA facilitated interviews and provided new perspectives. Jana and Levi Blankenship opened their home to me and offered much needed respite during my Hudson Valley research trips.

In Minnesota, I am most grateful to Alex Liebman, who originally reached out to me at a conference and invited me to meet farmers with whom he was working. I also wish to thank Jaime Villalaz and Rodrigo Cala at the Latino Economic Development Center in Minneapolis for facilitating multiple introductions and guiding me through the many fruitful regions of Latino/a farmers in the state. Much gratitude to Margot Higgins for welcoming me into her city and home while I worked in the Twin Cities.

I am tremendously appreciative of Colleen Donovan, formally of the Washington State University Small Farms Program, for inviting me to and hosting me in the state of Washington. Colleen, along with Marcia Ostrom, also of the Washington State University Small Farms Program, Katherine Selting Smith, who works with Viva Farms as part of the Northwest Small and Latino Farm Support program at Washington State University and Skagit County Extension, and José Limon and Crispin Garza at the FSA served as invaluable guides to the state's diverse immigrant growers, providing me with contacts, new perspectives, and much hope for the region. In all these regions, many other market managers, extension agents, and USDA staff assisted me along the way.

Numerous incredible student research assistants have worked with me to complete this project. They assisted me on site visits, transcribed, translated, and coded interviews, copyedited, organized my sources, wrote grant proposals, and helped me think through ideas. I have been beyond lucky to work with great students. At Goucher College, I worked with Sea Sloat and Sarah Meade, and at Syracuse University, I worked with Sara Andrea Quinteros-Fernández, Rebecca Jean Lustig, Fabiola Ortiz Valdez,

Briana Alfaro, Assata Cradle-Morgan, and Maizy Ludden. This book would not exist without their hard work and thoughtful contributions.

I am grateful to the funders that believed in this research and provided the resources to make it all possible, including the Environmental Studies Program at Goucher College, David B. Falk College of Sport and Human Dynamics at Syracuse University, the Labor Studies Working Group at Syracuse University, and the American Association of Geographers.

I am likewise grateful to the publishers that generously let me reprint portions of this research. Some sections of this work were previously printed in the edited volume *Food across Borders* (Rutgers University Press), and the journals *Agriculture and Human Values* and the *Journal of Peasant Studies*.

Many colleagues and mentors have helped me along this journey. This book's research trajectory started in graduate school, where my advisers Richard Walker, Nancy Peluso, Carolyn Finney, and Jake Kosek at the University of California at Berkeley all supported me through the beginning phases of this work, providing necessary theoretical frameworks and professional advice to get me where I am today. I am particularly grateful to Alison Hope Alkon, who not only served on my committee but also shared continuous friendship, in addition to mentorship on writing, publication, and generally surviving academia, as well as being my regular host when I return to California.

At Syracuse University, I am fortunate to have wonderful colleagues in the Food Studies Program: Evan Weissman, Anne Bellows, Rick Welsh, Elissa Johnson, Mary Kiernan, and Jennifer Hurley. I could not ask for a better group of people to work and share ideas and laugh with every day. Rick, in particular, has provided supportive and generous mentorship as I develop into a more established stage of my career, walking me through challenges, great and small. I am grateful to my dean, Diane Lyden Murphy, and everyone at Falk College for creating a compassionate environment to work in, encouraging my project as it developed, and being deeply supportive of working parents. Thank you also to Joseph Stoll, Syracuse University's cartographer, for making the maps that appear throughout this book.

This manuscript benefited from the collaborative feedback of many readers pervious to formal review. Clare Gupta and Lindsey Dillon read the first written iterations of this research, providing valuable perspective and support through the many professional and personal phases this project went through with me. Thank you to my collaborators on the *Food across*

Borders anthology, especially the editors, Don Mitchell, Melanie Dupuis, and Matthew Garcia, for their camaraderie and conversation on the early stages of drafting this book's core ideas. An extra thank you to Don, who casually came up with this book's title over coffee one day. I am grateful to Tore C. Olsson, Caela O'Connell, and their colleagues at the University of Tennessee Humanities Center at the University of Tennessee at Knoxville, who graciously invited me to present and receive feedback during their Food, Agriculture, and Society workshop. In the final writing phases, my writing group, consisting of Teresa Mares and David Meeks, shared extensive and critical feedback to help me get to the finish line. And finally, thank you to Beth Clevenger, Bob Gottlieb, Anthony Zannino, Virginia Crossman, Cindy Milstein, and everyone at the MIT Press as well as the formal reviewers for taking the interest and time to improve on this manuscript and create a book that I hope will be shared with a wide audience of readers, scholars, and activists.

During the time of starting this research and completing this manuscript, I gestated, gave birth to, and started the beginning stages of raising two amazing little girls. This was no easy feat, as the physical and emotional toll of parenting is more than I ever could have imagined. During this time, I also lost my mother. Yet I have had incredible support networks, and been held up by my family and friends, each step of the way. This book comes at what I hope is the end stretch of a challenging period of time on a personal level—one where my own goals were only made possible by the community around me as well as the generosity of friends far and near.

For a working parent, it could not be more important or valuable to know that your children are well loved and cared for when you go off to work every day. I could not have completed this book without the incredible care and support from the teachers and staff at Syracuse University's Early Education and Childcare Center. Everyone there made sure each moment I spent working on this book was without worry.

Thank you to my husband's family, Joyce Zern, Marc Zern, and Kathy Bacon-Greenberg, for stepping in when I traveled for research and conference presentations, and creating an extended support network for my children.

I am forever grateful to my father, Larry Minkoff, and my late mother, Rosemary Minkoff, for their everlasting love and support. Because of them, I have never questioned who I am and what I can accomplish. I am especially appreciative of my father, who continues to shower me with unconditional love, while making sure I always stay humble and grounded. I know my mother is reading this book somewhere, just waiting to tell me how proud she is and that it is just perfect (even though it surely is not).

Finally and most important, I am grateful for my little family each and every day. Thank you to my two daughters, Aviva and Mira, for consistently giving my work limits and meaning and helping me take myself less seriously. And thank you to Jonah for supporting my work from the beginning, being a true partner in every way, believing in my potential, and always making things work for our family. I could not be more proud and appreciative to be his partner.

1 From Farmworkers to Farm Owners: An Introduction

We wanted to name it Mariposa [farm] because ... do you know the story of the monarchs? The monarch butterflies? They need to fly from Mexico to Canada, [and] some of them die crossing the border to reach Canada. ... Some of the parents die during the trip, but the children know how to come back. I think that we as Latinos have a lot in common with the butterflies because in order to be here, we have to cross the borders, and sadly, a lot of times families lose their loved ones. But their children here, the children who are born here, always have the need of knowing their parent's' roots and always go looking for it.
—Marisela

I visited Mariposa Farm on a crisp spring day in March 2016, in a moment when the raw political divisions of rural America were on public display. Northwest Washington, like most regions of the country where fruit and vegetable production are the heart of the rural economy, is home to a large Latino/a population. Mostly of Mexican heritage, some are undocumented newcomers, while others are descendants of workers who came as part of the federal bracero guest worker program of the 1950s and 1960s. Almost all initially crossed the border looking for employment in the agricultural sector. Immigrant labor is crucial to the economic stability of this region. And as this book will describe, many of these immigrants are successfully rising in the ranks of food production and starting their own family-operated farms, living what many envision as the American dream. Yet signs in support of Donald Trump, a presidential candidate whose campaign centered on vitriol targeting immigrants, and Mexican immigrants in particular, lined the edges of the winding country roads of the Cascade Mountain foothills.

Figure 1.1
Beautiful greens display by Mariposa Farm at a market in Washington State.

The paradox of a rural America as a place that simultaneously provides opportunity even as it harbors a deeply ingrained and highly contradictory nativism plays out in the stories of Mexican immigrant farmers. As the above epigraph describes, out of economic desperation many people cross borders, seeking a new life. Yet what they find is that despite struggles, they are able to reroot their lives. It is not easy to be an immigrant in the United States, especially when you can be singled out for the color of your skin, stature of your body, or language on your lips. For most, day-to-day survival is enough. But for others, the memory of a life lived on land from which they harvested for their families, and the draw to the independence of growing one's own food and tasting familiar flavors, overpowers the feelings of exhaustion and defeat. The stories told in this book are of those who defy the odds, and in doing so, show us the way that a new America can flourish, if we are to accept and support them.

The Changing Face of American Agriculture

While the majority of US farm ownership remains in the hands of US-born people who identify as white, immigrants from Mexico, who identify as indigenous or mestizo, are gaining access to land and starting their own farm businesses. Many new farmers in the United States are immigrants, who initially came to the United States looking for work on others' farms. Using prior experience farming their own land in their home countries as well as recent experiences in the United States as migrant farmworkers, they transition to working on their own small-scale farms. As many Mexican farmers shift from working as laborers in others' fields to owning and operating their own businesses, they represent the new face of a flourishing generation of farmers.

Many of these farms reflect a vision of a multiracial and ecologically sustainable food system espoused by alternative food movement advocates. While Mexican immigrant farmers are certainly not a monolithic, organized, or self-identified group among US farmers, what this book describes are trends I saw throughout the country, as I followed distinct communities of immigrant workers in their paths to transition from positions as agricultural employees to circumstances where they controlled their own time, labor, and food-growing practices. In my research, I have found that throughout the United States, there are pockets of first-generation Mexican immigrant farmers who, unlike the majority of farmers in the United States, use a combination of what have been identified as alternative farming techniques. This includes simultaneously growing multiple crops (from four to hundreds), using integrated pest management techniques, maintaining small-scale production (ranging from three to eighty acres, with most between ten and twenty), employing mostly family labor, and selling directly at farmers markets to their local communities or regional wholesale distributors. Although not all farms fit this portrait completely—many hire some nonfamily labor, sell to wholesalers and in direct markets, and are not certified organic—these practices are reflective of farming approaches that are alternative to the dominant conventional industrial agriculture model.

Immigrant farmers are filling unmet gaps in knowledge and labor as they ascend to farm ownership in an economy where more and more US-born farmers are leaving midsize and small-scale farming, and failing to pass on their businesses to their children. They are entering farming in a

age → opportune
time

moment where nearly half of all farm operators in the United States are reaching retirement age (USDA 2014). Most farmers' children are not interested in taking on the family farm, as the labor input is high while profits are low and unstable. Further, there is already a higher demand than supply for organic food products in the United States, while consumer interest in organic and sustainably grown food continues to increase.[1] Immigrant farmers are migrating with agricultural expertise and skills, particularly experience in alterative growing practices, and are meeting this acute need for interested and willing American farmers.

In this book, I argue that immigrant farmers bring their knowledge and experience of alternative farming practices across the border, and despite challenges, are actively and substantially contributing to an alternative food system envisioned by food movement actors and activists. In order to understand how and why Mexican immigrant farmers have come to and created this niche, and what social and economic factors influence their practices, I explore the following questions: Why are immigrant farmworkers starting their own farms, despite enormous challenges? What is the historic context that has determined their position in the current agrifood system? How does their race, ethnicity, and citizenship status affect their agricultural practices and agrarian identity? What does their transition from workers to owners mean for more just labor in the fields? Finally, I investigate their role in today's growing alternative agrifood movements, asking what these findings mean for scholars and activists trying to understand resistance to our industrial agriculture model and agrarian class transition on a global scale. I discuss the importance of recognizing immigrant farmers of color, and their vast and diverse knowledge for the ecological and social sustainability of our food system as a whole. Through the lens of global agrarian transition, I look at the unacknowledged centrality of race, ethnicity, and immigration to transnational changes in our food system.

I draw on research with Mexican immigrant farmers in the United States along with the state and nonstate actors who work with them, exploring the relationship between class transitions, race, and migration in agriculture today. I define a farmer foremost as someone who identifies themselves as a farmer (campesino, ranchero, or *agricultor*, in Spanish)—more specifically as one who currently owns their farm business, to differentiate them from a farm laborer working under an employer. Most rented the land they cultivated, although some owned it, and all performed at least some of the manual labor on the farm. They have been operating their own farms in the United States for a range of two to twenty years, with a minority simultaneously working other jobs, some in farmwork, and others in construction. All the farmers made at least some, if not all, of their income from their own farming businesses.[2]

All farmers emigrated from Mexico, and identify as Latino/a or Hispanic.[3] In Washington and California, many farmers interviewed also identify as Triqui or Mixteco (indigenous to Mexico).[4] Most speak limited English, with Spanish being their first language. For some who speak indigenous languages, Spanish is also a second language. Some have English-speaking children who are teenagers or young adults, and help with translation for forms or at the market. I interviewed adult children in a few instances, sometimes in addition to their parents' interviews.

Besides the typical challenges of becoming a new farmer, which include lack of access to start-up capital, land, labor, and markets, immigrant farmers must contend with their citizenship status, race, and ethnicity as well as linguistic, literacy, and educational limitations. As immigrants, and particularly as immigrants of color, participants' experience of US citizenship varies. Many immigrant farmers are undocumented. US immigration and border policy make it nearly impossible for most farmworkers to enter the United States legally. Additionally, increased militarization at the US-Mexican border, and the resulting danger and cost of crossing the border, discourage seasonal migrations, encouraging people to develop stronger communities and secure livelihoods on one side (Holmes 2013). This increases their desire to subsist in the United States more permanently, which for those in this study means using their skills as farmers to move up the food labor chain from farmworker to farm operator. Yet undocumented farmers are ineligible for any government-sponsored agricultural support programs, such as those available through the USDA.

Although many farmers interviewed did have documents to legally live and work in the United States, their ease and opportunity in accessing land and support to farm was still significantly affected by their racialized identity. For those who are documented and therefore able to apply for government assistance, such as USDA loans, the inability to read, write, or understand the required forms necessary to become established farmers in the United States can prove challenging. Immigrant farmers' language skills, literacy abilities, and education levels vary. Most have had little, if any, formal education, while others have completed elementary or high school, and speak some English. Yet even they are intimidated by the bureaucracy of the US agriculture system, and frequently lack the level of written organizational skills necessary to record and quantify their farming practices and apply for support.

I have found that this particular set of farmers challenges not only class, racial, and citizenship-based hierarchies in US agriculture but also exemplify how race and culture matter in the formation of agricultural practices and social relations. This book explicates immigrants' food and farming practices as a consequence of racial and citizenship-based exclusion as well as immigrants' struggle to redefine their relationship to land and cultural practice in a new country. On the one hand, they are discriminated against for their race and citizenship status, leaving them with little capital to start farming, and limited options in terms of land and market access. On the other hand, they express a preference for farming in a particular style—one where they are able to regain control over their daily labor and reproduce a specific agrarian way of life, defying linear capitalist agrarian development.

Industrial farming, including monocropping, heavy synthetic inputs, wholesale markets, and a low-paid nonfamily workforce, would make rational economic sense to immigrant farmers as perhaps the most direct path to agrarian class mobility. Yet racial exclusions constrain immigrants' options as farmers, therefore limiting them to particular forms of cultivation. All nonwhite immigrants in the United States progressing from worker to owner, including Japanese, Chinese, and Sikh farmers, have had to overcome obstacles based on not only class but also racial, ethnic, and varying degrees of citizenship status, in addition to their linguistic, literary, and educational limitations. Due to compounded marginalization by racist and classist legal structures, immigrant farmers of color have fewer financial resources, and less access to land, inputs, capital, and markets, than their white counterparts (Garcia 2002; Minkoff-Zern et al. 2011; Matsumoto 1993; Chan 1989; Wells 1996). Even when farmers of color succeed in climbing the agricultural ladder, their social positioning means that they do so with limited resources and varying levels of success.

Additionally, many immigrant farmers actively choose farming more small-scale, diverse cropping systems, with limited synthetic inputs and mostly family labor. This form of farming, although not purely subsistence, allows them to reclaim control over their own labor and livelihoods, while also earning a cash income (see Welsh 1997). This farming approach is both a means of survival and way of resisting the dominant mode of global agricultural development, and can only be fully understood through an analysis of race, citizenship, and migration. Although these explanations might seem contradictory—with one based in limitations, and the other based in preference—these findings exemplify the complexities of present-day agricultural transitions, where racial positioning and the political economy of migration must be brought to the center of agrarian analysis.

Alternative Farming: Certifications, Standards, and Identities

There are many labels used to identify farmers who use alternative cultivation practices. Some are more clearly defined than others. "Organic," for example, is a term regulated by the USDA as well as several third-party certifiers. "Biodynamic," a stricter standard for ecological farming, is also strictly defined, although only by a nonprofit certifier. On the other end of the spectrum, the terms "alternative," "local," and "natural" have neither a certification process nor national-scale official standards. I use the term "alternative farming/production" to broadly imply that these immigrant farmers are growing in a way that does not fit within standard agro-industrial practices. I recognize this is an imperfect term, as inclusion in alternative food movements is contested, and there is no clear definition of practices.

Despite lacking standard or agreed-on definitions, there are certainly large national and global movements of actors that coalesce around these terms, or identities, some of which are conflicting and at times confrontational in their goals. Yet as David Goodman, E. Melanie DuPuis, and Michael Goodman (2012, 4) describe below, those that distinguish themselves as part of a universal alternative food movement commonly identify in opposition to the global industrial food system, which they see as largely "unsustainable":

> In their general problematic, alternative food networks and the fair trade movement have emerged in response to the glaring and multifaceted contradictions of the unsustainable industrial food system and the exploitative trading relations embedded in the global supply chains that support its growth and (expanded) reproduction. ... [A]ctivists are mapping different ways forward by creating new economic and cultural spaces for the trading, production, and consumption of food—organic, fair trade, local, quality, "slow"—whose ethical and esthetic

alternative "qualifications" distinguish them from the products conventionally supplied by international trade, mainstream food manufacturers, and supermarket chains.

Goodman and his colleagues also point to what is seen by many activists and academics as the contradictory nature of many alternative food movement actors and initiatives: they are identifying as alternative to an industrial system of producing food that is destructive to our environmental resources, social equality, cultural fabric, and human right to food, and yet the alternative being suggested is still capitalist in nature and therefore ultimately will reproduce many of the same problems. They suggest the "politics of alternative food system-making as a process" rather than a designation where one deems food and food-related practices as either "good" or "bad."

Labor, in particular, is a central contradiction I have had to contend with as I look at how racialized workers reclaim the means of production in the most basic terms, gaining control over their own physical labor, while also reproducing the same labor structure as their farm businesses grow. The question of labor justice looms large and is in no way solved by workers starting their own farms, as I discuss in chapter 5. I have seen only a few examples of Mexican farmers creating a more cooperative labor structure; most farmers were adamantly averse to this idea when I brought it up. Although Mexican immigrant farmers do not solve the problem of labor injustice simply by their existence, as I explore below, I still see their persistence and growing presence as a sign of positive changes in US agriculture as a whole, both in terms of racial justice and ecological sustainability.

Following Goodman and his colleagues' suggestion (and acknowledging the inherent messiness of labor politics on immigrant farms), I contend that alternative food movements, which have largely left out farmworkers and farmers of color (see, among others, Alkon and Agyeman 2011; Allen 2004; Gray 2013; Guthman 2014), must expand on their efforts at inclusion by utilizing a reflexive approach to alternative food movement building. To do so, farmer identities must be challenged to include farmers of color as well as bridge the divide between former workers and farm owner/operators. For this to happen, white farmers and consumers will first have to face the exclusionary nature of alternative food movements, and be willing to recognize the diversity of races and ethnicities present in farming today. Building on the diversity of alternative farmers and farming can only function to strengthen the movement, bridging class- and race-based divides in the effort to resist corporate food regimes. In this book, I discuss the ways that immigrant farmers utilize alternative farming practices, and the relationship between their farming practices and their racial and ethnic identities, making the case for a more inclusive alternative food movement.

A Hidden Population

According to official USDA census data, the number of farms with principal operators (the person who manages the farm, not necessarily the business owner or landowner) of "Spanish, Hispanic, or Latino origin" grew from 50,592 in 2002 to 55,570 in 2007.[5] In 2012, the number increased again, to 67,000 farms, for a 21 percent increase over five years. Of those 67,000 farm operators of Latino/a origin, the vast majority (64,439) were the primary farm business owners as well (USDA 2014).[6] In other words, Latino/as are increasingly assuming leadership roles on farms in the United States. Even as the census shows increasing numbers, as I discuss in chapter 2, the number of Latino/a immigrant farmers is undoubtedly still undercounted by this measure due to the distrust of the government, lack of mainstream farming practices, and linguistic, cultural, and social barriers to agricultural institutions.

Related to the lack of accurate data and tracking, the existence of Mexican and other Latino/a immigrant farmers is often unknown or overlooked in day-to-day, on-the-ground USDA operations. In beginning research with immigrant farmers, I made unannounced phone calls to USDA regional headquarters across the United States in all five states included in this study, including California, Virginia, New York, Washington, and Minnesota. In each case, when I first called and asked to speak to someone who works with "Latino or Latina farmers," the person on the end of the line responded as if I had asked about Latino/a *farmworkers*, not farm business owners. I consistently had to explain, "I am looking to speak with someone in your office who might work with immigrant *farmers*, as in farm business owners, not laborers." Even in regions where immigrant farmers exist in significant numbers, it took substantial explanation to start a conversation in which USDA staff understood the specific group of farmers that I was interested in discussing. They were either unaware that Mexican and other immigrant farmers existed in their region, or were so accustomed to thinking of

Mexican immigrants as agricultural workers that they disregarded their encounters with immigrant farmers until probed directly.

This lack of awareness among USDA staff about Mexican and other Latino/a immigrant farmers is reflected in the scholarly literature on Latino/as in agriculture in the United States. There is a growing body of geographic, anthropological, and sociological research on farm labor that critically engages with the politically produced vulnerability as well as exploitation of the immigrant body. This literature contributes to our understanding of historical and modern-day labor conditions in the agrifood system—an understanding that is necessary for gaining a comprehensive picture of the political economy of food production and advocating for workers' rights throughout the food system. In particular, this work investigates the relationship between the Latino/a immigrant worker and the state, providing nuanced analysis of how US national policy and immigration agencies reinforce unjust working conditions along with a racialized workforce (see, among others, Allen 2008; Brown and Getz 2008; Guthman and Brown 2016; Gray 2013; Harrison 2011; Holmes 2013; Mitchell 1996; Sbicca 2015). Yet most critical analysis of immigrant workers thus far does not include the possibility that some immigrant workers are in fact advancing in this agrarian class system. Further, there has been almost no comprehensive inquiry of how immigrant farm owners are experiencing state apparatuses.[7]

Additionally, there has been a recent proliferation of scholars researching and writing about race and agrifood systems, particularly through the lens of food justice in the United States. Such work has investigated how race matters in the context of modern-day food movements, food access, and labor hierarchies. Much of this research, as well as my own work, is grounded in the notion of racial formations. Racial formations, which occur through a process of "historically situated projects in which human bodies and social structures are represented and organized" (Omi and Winant 2014, 55–56), are imposed and reinforced via power relations within the US food and agricultural system. The relationship between racial formations and agrifood systems has been discussed in the context of agricultural regulations (Minkoff-Zern 2014c), labor (Mitchell 1996; Garcia 2002; Walker 2004), inclusion in and access to markets (Alkon 2008; Slocum and Saldanha 2013; Slocum 2007), the inclusion (or lack thereof) in so-called alternative food movements (Alkon and Agyeman 2011; Alkon and McCullen 2011; Allen 2004; Allen et al. 2003; Guthman 2008a, 2008b;

Harper 2010), and farmer-led US-based movements (Brent, Schiavoni, and Alonso-Fradeja 2015; Minkoff-Zern 2014a). Yet, none of this literature specifically looks at immigrant farmers and their increasing presence in US agriculture. This book makes a needed intervention, exploring how immigrant farmers interact with the state, markets, and agrarian social networks in the United States.

Immigrant Farmers and Their Supporters

Over the course of five years, with the support of eight research assistants, including undergraduate and graduate students from Goucher College and Syracuse University, I interviewed over seventy immigrant farmers in five distinct regions of the United States. Semistructured interviews with farmers took place at their farms, homes, and farmers markets. I also conducted participant observation at farms and farmers markets where Latino/a farmers were prevalent as well as attended a six-month training course for new farmers that was geared toward immigrant farmworkers. To meet farmers, I attended relevant conferences and markets where immigrant farmers sell their goods. I also met farmers through other immigrant farmers, farmer training/incubator organizations, extension agents, USDA staff, farmers market managers, and other groups that outreach to immigrant farmers. Most interviews with farmers were in Spanish, and were transcribed and translated by myself or a student research assistant.

In addition to farmers, I interviewed people who interacted with and outreached to Mexican and immigrant farmers as part of their jobs. This includes twenty-seven employees of nonstate or not-for-profit programs, six university extension agents, and fourteen USDA staff members. In some cases, I was also able to observe them during interactions with farmers. Through these interviews and observations, I was able to gain a broader perspective on what kinds of challenges and opportunities immigrant farmers face, particularly in terms of access to land and markets, federal and state resources, certification programs, and regional agricultural networks and associations.

The interviews at nonprofit programs included individuals who advocate for and work with immigrant and other low-resource farmers, including staff at farm incubators and training programs, food hubs, produce brokerages, marketing collectives, farmers market management, and industry

commissions. Many of these organizations are explicitly focused on helping the Latino/a immigrant community advance in agricultural careers and
food system opportunities in their regions, such as the Minneapolis-based
Latino Economic Development Center and Sunnyside Transformation of
Yakima Valley in Washington State. Staff at these organizations spoke with
me about creating market opportunities for immigrant farmers, and assisting them with business, language, and literacy skills. When I met with representatives from farmer training and incubator programs, they similarly
emphasized market access as well as business and language skills, but were
also focused on helping farmers with land access and adjusting to farming techniques suited to the regions. Farmers market managers were not as
directly invested in the success of Latino/a farmers, and some even exhib-
ited their own bias against them. Yet all the market managers worked closely
with immigrant farmers and had become personally interested in seeing
them succeed, albeit at varying levels. They discussed going on farm visits,
helping them with their marketing, signage, and packaging, and assisting
them with certification and market-required paperwork as well as the ways
they struggled in competing with their white counterparts.

On a national level, I met with organizations such as the Rural Coalition
and the National Latino Farmer and Ranchers Trade Association that lobby
on behalf of immigrant and Latino/a farmers. Drawing on their agrarian
policy advocacy work, they were able to speak to the discrimination that
farmers are experiencing across the country and in particular their treatment at the USDA, which is the subject of chapter 3.

Government employees included extension and outreach agents from
land-grant universities and USDA agents/staff members. Extension and outreach agents from state universities who specialize in small farms generally
had a good sense of the immigrant farming community. They are often the
first line of entry for farmers to access markets, land, training programs,
and grants, especially in areas where there is no farm training or incubator program. In New York, Washington, and Virginia, university extension
introduced me to many of the farmers I later interviewed. At the USDA,
I met with the Natural Resources Conservation Service (NRCS) and Farm
Service Agency (FSA) at the local and state levels, when available. They discussed what resources were available to farmers, and their offices' level of
outreach to the local immigrant farming community, including their limitations related to outreach.

On the federal level, I interviewed staff members who work in the Office of Advocacy and Outreach with the Socially Disadvantaged Farmers and Ranchers Program. I also interviewed staff members who worked on the USDA's Hispanic Farmers and Ranchers discrimination suit and claims process. In 2000, a class action suit was filed against the USDA on behalf of Hispanic farmers and ranchers who were discriminated against from 1981 to 2000 while applying for USDA loans. The USDA admitted to discrimination, and this case was settled via a claims process, where farmers were eligible to receive from $50,000 to $250,000 (Hispanic and Women Farmers and Ranchers Claims and Resolution Process 2012; Martinez and Gomez 2011). Staff discussed with me how this process worked and what it means for Latino/a farmers today.

Through this set of interviews and meetings, I gained a bird's-eye view of what Mexican immigrant farmers are up against as well as what opportunities and support systems are in place to help them succeed. Of course, it was through speaking to farmers themselves that I heard the most moving stories and personalized perspectives on how they plow the paths they are creating. By listening to individuals in open-ended interviews as well as taking time to walk farmers' lands and see their crops, kitchen tables, and marketplaces, I was able to grasp a sense of people's lived experiences as immigrant farmers in the United States today. Certainly, there are limitations to doing interview-based research. While I conducted over one hundred interviews in total, it is difficult to create a thorough quantitative analysis of them given that each discussion took its own form, and in these meetings, stories were privileged over checking boxes.[8] Below I explore the differing geographic spaces they are working in, with their varied challenges and prospects, and the route I took into each of these regions.

Finding Sites and Meeting Farmers

The geographically diverse case studies included in this book provide a sample of distinct clusters of Mexican immigrant farmers in the United States. Large numbers of immigrants migrate to these areas, as they contain a high percentage of fruit and vegetable farms, requiring a large labor force. As farmworkers transition to growers, they also tend to concentrate on fruit and vegetable production, in part because the capital required to enter the market is lower for fruits and vegetables than other crops.[9] These regions provide access to urban markets for direct produce sales as well, which I have found immigrant growers prefer due to the ability to sell smaller amounts of diverse products with less bureaucracy, as I discuss more in chapter 3. Three out of five of the regions had farmer training programs and/or farm business incubator projects, which had a purposeful emphasis on immigrant farmers, and helped farmers learn cultivation techniques and business skills for farming in the United States as well as assisted them in land and market acquisition. These regions are distinct in that they vary in their seasonality, the size of the general Latino/a immigrant population, and the length of time the immigrant communities have been established in the region.

I began this course of inquiry as part of my dissertation research as a graduate student at the University of California at Berkeley in 2011. My dissertation research looked at the condition and contradictions of farmworker food insecurity along California's Central Coast, investigating how farmworkers coped with lacking access to adequate food and nutrition. As an outsider to the farmworker community, I was initially surprised by how many farmworkers I interviewed were in the process of starting their own gardens and farms. Yet when I further reflected on this, it made a lot of sense. The workers I interviewed came from agrarian backgrounds and were skilled at many elements of farm labor, not just the repetitive tasks they were assigned as workers in California's industrial agriculture system. Further, they longed for the foods they missed from back home as well as the time spent cultivating land with family, which dramatically differed from the piecemeal assignments they fulfilled in their daily work on large-scale monocropped fields as pickers and packers.

Although most of these farmworkers were early in the process of starting farms, taking farmer business training courses, renting their first plots of land, or just beginning to sell crops grown in a community garden, I saw the ways they were succeeding, despite an extremely uphill battle. When I started discussing the presence of farmworkers turned farmers with labor advocates, agrarian scholars, white farmers, and others with broad knowledge of the agriculture industry, most thought what I was seeing made up a small group, and had no confidence in these farmers' ability to succeed, given financial, cultural, linguistic, and citizenship-based obstacles. Their doubt was in part what motivated me to pursue this research. From

Figure 1.2
Map of California region of research.

what I was observing, there was a larger group than most outsiders could imagine, and these farmers were not going to give up easily.

With geographic market access to the San Francisco Bay Area and surrounding wealthy cities, rich and well-drained soil, and a year-round productive climate, the northern Central Coast seems like an ideal place to start a new produce farm. This region is popular for aspiring and beginning farmers, especially the commonly young, white, college-educated graduates of the University of California at Santa Cruz's apprenticeship program in agroecology and sustainable food systems. Yet farming in this region can be challenging, even for beginning farmers who have resources and capital with which to start. In terms of succeeding at farming for profit, the competition is stiff, with saturated markets in the prosperous urban areas.

Contrary to its image as a haven for local and organic food, the region is actually dominated by conventional strawberry and lettuce growing, which has prevailed for decades. It is in these conventional fields that most immigrant farmers begin and eventually work their way out to start small organic farms. The Agriculture and Land-Based Training Association (ALBA) training program is geared toward farmworkers and other limited-resource aspiring farmers in Salinas, California.[10] It is through this training program, which includes a six-month course as well as access to rented land and machinery after graduation, that many immigrant farmers get a foothold in this competitive market.

Most of the immigrant farmers I met in California had participated in this program, which has existed for about twenty years and has had a large influence on the ascendance of farmworkers to farm ownership in

Figure 1.3
Sign at the entrance to ALBA.

the area. The organization promotes organic methods as well as diversified production, and assists farmers with obtaining organic certification, which is reflected in the practices of the farmers I interviewed. Although direct marketing is the preference of many of these farmers, entry for new farmers into farmers markets with high-paying customers is difficult, and newer farmers in this area sell primarily to produce brokers.

ALBA graduates are certainly not the only Mexican or immigrant farmers in the region, though, as many second- and third-generation Mexicans have entered conventional strawberry production too. The California Strawberry Commission (2014) reports that 85 percent of strawberry growers in the state are now of Latino/a or Asian descent, and the commission recently elected its first Latina chair. As the industry faces attacks from consumers and activist groups for poor labor practices along with increased, controversial pesticide use, it proudly promotes this immigrant population to create a new image for the crop. I did not interview these farmers, as they are primarily second- and third-generation immigrants, yet they do provide a particular kind of counterpoint to the trends I am seeing, as I discuss more in chapter 6.[11]

When I moved to the East Coast for a postdoctoral position at Goucher College in Baltimore, Maryland, I started seeking out immigrant farmers in my area. Due to my proximity to Washington, DC, I looked into federally funded immigrant and refugee programs, with offices in the nation's capital. I learned about the Refugee Agricultural Partnership Program, sponsored through the Office of Refugee Resettlement, and was able to meet with the director at the time, Larry Laverentz. He confirmed my speculation: Mexican immigrant farmers are everywhere, if you know how to find them. He sent me to the regional farmers markets, where market managers connected me with a sizable community of Latino/a farmers on the Northern Neck of Virginia who traveled weekly to the DC area to sell their products.

Situated between the Potomac and Rappahannock Rivers, the Northern Neck is one of three peninsulas (or "necks") that jut out into the Chesapeake Bay. The "Neck" is representative of a pattern of out-migration throughout the rural South. As white agrarian communities struggle to retain their youth, new immigrant populations are ascending both culturally and economically (Kasarda and Johnson 2006; Zandt 2014). This migration of white youth is an opportunity for immigrant farmers to enter the agricultural market.

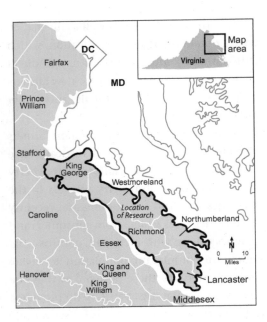

Figure 1.4
Map of Virginia region of research.

There are approximately thirty immigrant families farming on the Neck, almost all part of an extended family from Jalisco, Mexico. Although most of the area is cultivated by corn, wheat, and soybean growers, immigrant farmers represent one-half to two-thirds of the fruit and vegetable farmers on the northern peninsula, according to estimates by farmers themselves as well as local USDA and extension staff. These farmers mostly sell directly to customers at markets in Washington, DC, and the nearby suburbs in northern Virginia. There is no farmer training program in this region, and the immigrant farmer population has sprung up by its own volition, as multiple generations of Mexican immigrants came here following the East Coast berry harvest. It is easier to start farming here than in California, as water is more plentiful, land is more affordable and easy to access, and markets for direct produce sales are less saturated. Although these farmers are not certified organic, they are still growing diversified crops, and using low-spray and integrated pest management techniques.

As my own career progressed, and I moved locations, finally to central New York, where I currently work at Syracuse University, I looked for the same kind of local farming population in my proximity. Due to the dominance of the dairy industry and high start-up costs to purchase the required infrastructure, there are few Mexican or other Latino/a farmers in the region. Instead, I explored a research site in the Hudson Valley, an agricultural zone with more prevalent fruit and vegetable production as well as better access to direct markets in New York City.

In the Hudson Valley, I met farmers through the FARMroots' Beginning Farmer Program, an aspiring farmer training program organized by a farmers market association based in New York City. Focused on "sustainable farming," the program was created in 2000 as a partnership between Greenmarket and Cornell Cooperative Extension to support new farmers in New York City, the Hudson Valley and Catskill regions, and New Jersey and northeastern Pennsylvania. At its inception, the program focused on the immigrant population in the region, helping new farmers access land and resources, although it has broadened its mission since. As the program is based under the larger umbrella of a farmers market organization, most farmers I met in this region were selling directly to customers at markets in New York City.

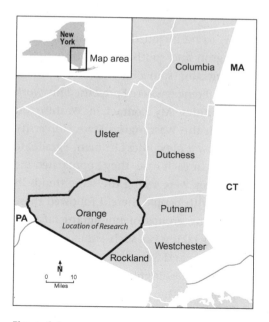

Figure 1.5
Map of New York State region of research.

Many of the farmers in this program found land to rent in the "black dirt" region of the Hudson Valley, which got its name from its dark and fertile soil, a remnant of a glacial lake and regular flooding of the adjacent Wallkill River. Until recently, it was a popular area for onion farming, with good access to New York City markets, and soil that was particularly favorable to the crop. Onions were cultivated by Polish and German immigrants and their descendants through the twentieth century. Today, with incoming pressures from agritourism, and the proximity of the area to New York City as a second-home destination, combined with the fact that the onion market has shifted, the area is struggling to maintain its agricultural backbone. I found immigrant farmers growing on land nestled between larger farms and estates, sometimes in the middle of others' fields, wherever they could get hold of property. This small group of Latino/a farmers are recent inhabitants of the region, which does not have as long an established history of Latino/a immigrant community as the other areas in the study. Not fitting with the local farming culture of monocropped rows as well as heavily sprayed and weedless fields, these farmers were often targeted by locals for their "messy" cultivation strategies and seen as unwelcome outsiders.

The last two sites, or case studies, to be included in my project were in northwestern and central Washington and southeastern Minnesota. I traveled to each of these sites after meeting someone who worked with immigrant farming communities at conferences where I presented my work on farmworker turned farmer communities. My contact in Washington was Colleen Donovan, who works with the Washington State University Extension, and my contact in Minnesota was Alexander Liebman, a graduate student at the University of Minnesota. In each case, they approached me after my presentation to tell me that they were seeing the same trends in their area and that I should come talk with people there. I followed these leads and was thrilled to see the thriving groups of immigrant farmers, working with the same challenges and taking on such similar kinds of agrarian practices as in California, Virginia, and New York.

Immigrant farmers in northwestern Washington also benefit from a farmer training and incubator program. The program, Viva Farms, is specifically focused on training the local farmworker population to fill what the organizers see as gaps in the local agricultural workforce, as the region's white farmers retire. Similar to California's northern Central Coast, the area

Figure 1.6
Map of Washington State region of research.

is well known for its berry production. Given its scenic location between the Cascade Range and Puget Sound, with a mild year-round climate, northwestern Washington's agricultural region is at constant threat of residential development. Maintaining a thriving agricultural economy is a challenge, and American Farmland Trust designated the region the fifth most threatened agricultural area in the nation. With rich soils and good access to Seattle-area markets, which are less saturated than those in California down the coast, northwestern Washington is a somewhat-welcoming place for immigrants to enter the market. Most farmers I interviewed here focused on direct markets, primarily farmers markets and restaurant sales.

Additionally, Mexican immigrants have been in the area for many generations, dating back to the Bracero Program. Similar to California, Washington also has a sizable group of Mexican farmers who do not fit the alternative farming mold. In addition to the alternative farmers in northwestern Washington, I interviewed six first-generation immigrant orchardists in central Washington who had each bought a conventional fruit orchard from their previous employer. They do not use the description of growing techniques discussed in this book as closely as the diversified growers who make up the majority of the study. This immigrant farming population, although statistically significant based on state-level USDA reports, are an anomaly according to my national study. In these cases, the workers must be documented in order to access federal loans, which are necessary given the high capital inputs required to operate these farms. They also buy the farms at below-market rates and are dependent on the goodwill of their employers to sell to them. This is not to say they do not have a place in my analysis; I discuss their situation in more detail in chapter 6. Throughout the book, however, I refer primarily to the diversified growers who make up the majority of my interview population.

Southeast Minnesota, my final case study, had the least in common with the other regions I visited. Generally a commodity crop region, where most of the agricultural land is planted in corn and soy, the Latino/a population is more populous in urban areas. Yet there is some fruit and vegetable production, and where there is produce, there are farmworkers. In this region, the Latino Economic Development Center, an urban organization, identified a niche for Latino/a growers as part of its larger mission to help Latino/as in Minnesota become successful business owners and local community leaders. Seeing how many of their community members had agricultural experience from their home countries and their employment in the United States, they have made agriculture part of their central focus and have begun to help interested members find land in the area. It has been a struggle economically, as they are still new to understanding the local agricultural market. Many of the farmers they work with sell through a cooperative marketing collective, which concentrates on immigrant farmers. They have also teamed up with local food hubs and other organizations that assist them in finding facilities for washing and packing as well as avenues to market their products. Given that farmers are coming together around an urban hub rather than a rural one, as is the case in the other sites, the farms are more spread out across the state, with one farm located far to the northwest of the others.

While these case studies are in no way comprehensive of all of the Latino/a immigrant farmers successfully cultivating in the United States, and I have surely left out some very significant regions, I believe by looking

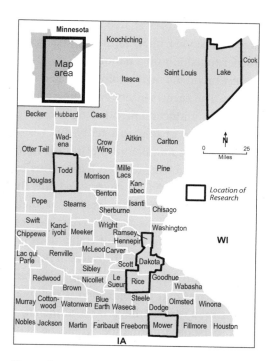

Figure 1.7
Map of Minnesota region of research.

at these five distinct areas of production, I have been able to capture an idea of the challenges and possibilities for immigrant farmers today.

A Few Notes on Method and Procedure

The sites I examined and people I interviewed for this study were chosen in part as a measure of convenience, based on my personal location at the time, and in part in relation to individuals I met along the way, and where they helped me make connections—a snowball sampling of regions and people. Additionally, with the exception of the farmers I started working with during my dissertation in California and have continuing relationships with over many years, I was only able to meet, observe, and interview most farmers once or twice for a few hours, at their farm, and for some, at the market as well. The downside is that I wasn't able to build a relationship separate from the individual who introduced me, and so to be fair, that could have skewed what kind of information they shared with me. Alternately, the benefit is that I was able to interview many farmers and develop a broad sense of this worker-to-owner transition on a national scale.

And finally, I'd like to offer a reflection on my methodology and decision to maintain the anonymity of farmers. The farmers interviewed are a mix of resident aliens, naturalized citizens, and undocumented immigrants who have been in the United States for a range of four to twenty-five years. Most of the farmers who are documented came before the Immigration Reform and Control Act (IRCA) of 1986, which provided legal status to undocumented immigrants who arrived before 1982. I never asked directly about farmers' documentation status, but through the telling of their stories, I could often discern whether participants were documented or not. Because this information makes them potentially vulnerable research participants, at risk of deportation, throughout most of the research process I made the assumption that they would want to be kept anonymous. As part of receiving the permission to conduct research through the institutional review boards at the various universities where I have been affiliated, I stated that immigrant participants' personal information would be kept confidential. This was meant to provide protection for the participants.

Yet as my research continued, I found that many farmers did not want to remain anonymous. As small business owners, they wanted their names used and sought to promote their farms. Even undocumented farmers, who volunteered their immigration status, asked me to use their real name. Only while conducting the final leg of research did I fully realize how many farmers actually wished to be recognized by name. This could have resulted from the fact that only toward the end of the study did I introduce the project by stating that I was writing a book. I believe the notion of a book grounds the project for participants in that there is to be a tangible and shareable outcome of the interviews rather than the vague notion of "research." In the last year of my research, I changed my process with the institutional review board, giving participants the option to have their name used or to be anonymous. Then as I began writing this book, Trump was elected president and brought in an administration that claims to be committed to purging the United States of all undocumented immigrants. Given this current state of affairs, I ultimately chose to keep all immigrants' names anonymous, documented or not, so as to create the most possible protection. This decision has been a difficult one, since some farmers were clear that I should use their names. But when those interviews were conducted, we were living in another era for immigrants in the United States, and I do not want to assume they would feel the same if I asked them the same question regarding their identity today.[12]

Book Organization

In chapter 2, "Sharecroppers, Braceros, and 'Illegals': Racializing the Agricultural Ladder," I look at the intellectual history of structural discrimination against farm laborers in the United States, and how this history has set the groundwork for the challenges that immigrant farmers and other farmers of color face in advancing economically and socially in US agriculture today. From the institution of slavery to domestic and international policies such as the Bracero Program and North American Trade Agreement (NAFTA), people of color have been relegated to an economically and socially disadvantaged role in US agriculture. Concurrently, white farmers have been awarded privileges that give them advantages in establishing landownership as well as accessing capital and markets. I bring this history up to date with a discussion of the treatment and expectations for immigrants currently laboring in agricultural communities and spaces. Utilizing the commonly cited metaphor of the agricultural ladder, this chapter establishes a base for understanding the particular challenges that Latino/a immigrant farmers face today.

"Institutions, Standardization, and Markets: Hungry for Opportunity in US Agriculture," the third chapter, investigates how Latino/a immigrant farmers navigate USDA programs, university extension services, and other agricultural opportunities, which often necessitate standardizing farming practices and accepting bureaucracy for participation. This chapter shows how Latino/a immigrant farmers' agrarian norms and practices are at odds with institutional requirements for agrarian standardization. I argue that immigrant farming practices and racialized identities are frequently unseen by, and illegible to, the state, university, and other research opportunities as well as alternative food institutions and marketplaces. This disjuncture leads to the increased racial exclusion of immigrant farmers from conventional and alternative agrarian opportunities today. Most agrarian-based organizations and institutions have failed to acknowledge this schism between rural Latino/a immigrants, the state, and agricultural institutions, thereby inhibiting a meaningful transition in the fields and continuing a legacy of unequal access to agrarian opportunities for nonwhite immigrant farmers.

In the fourth chapter, "Food, Identity, and Agricultural Practice: Recreating Home through the Family Farm," Latino/a farmers' ability to reclaim land and succeed as farmers in the United States is constantly being defined as well as redefined in relation to racial, ethnic, and socioeconomic hierarchies. This chapter employs the complex notions of home, identity, and place to understand how and why immigrant farmworkers are farming in the United States, despite particular challenges based on their racial and ethnic social positioning. I argue that the rationale and motivation of immigrant farmers in the United States can only be understood through the lens of identity, as their challenges as well as motivations are unique to their racialized and ethnic social status. I discuss both alternative and conventional farming practices embraced by immigrant farmers, looking at how these approaches compare as they strive to build an agrarian livelihood. In this chapter, I show the ways these farmers are re-creating a new sense of home through cultivation and consumption practices, ultimately proposing that it is these connections to an agrarian identity that keep them farming, despite the difficulties.

In chapter 5, "Shifting the Means of Production: Food Sovereignty, Labor, and the Freedom to Farm," I discuss immigrant farmers' drive for autonomy from their former bosses, and what their success might mean for the future of agrarian class relations. I look at the ways that their accomplishments as small-scale and diversified famers fit within the global movement for food sovereignty from industrial food system, despite their aversion to engaging with social movement politics. I also address the contradictions these farms represent in terms of agricultural labor inequality, as immigrant farmers epitomize both a racial and ethnic transition in US agriculture, and the limitations to reforming a historically unjust class system. And I examine what this racial and ethnic transition in farming means for larger questions of global agrarian transition.

Finally, in chapter 6, "The Rain Falls for Every Farmer: Growing Ecological and Social Diversity," I turn to the more pragmatic task of presenting suggestions for USDA, university extension, and alternative food movement practice and policy. Exploring how policy makers and social movement actors can best support immigrant farmers, I incorporate these recommendations with a critical analysis of identity politics within

US food movements. I look closely at Latino/a immigrant farming practices, arguing that although they farm using practices that are deemed sustainable or ecological by alternative food movement standards, the alternative food movement has not yet recognized their increasing potential for contributing to the agroecological knowledge base on US farms. I make the case for a deeper look into who is included and excluded from alternative farming movements and spaces, and importance of creating new opportunities for immigrant farmers of color as part of these social networks and markets.

2   Sharecroppers, Braceros, and "Illegals": Racializing the Agricultural Ladder

> My boss is white, and I told him, "How many whites do you see working here? It's because of the Mexicans that you guys are at the top. If you didn't have Mexicans, you would go down." ... I think there are always going to be the racist folks who think we ought to just be working for them or whatever, instead of trying to have our place or own business.
>
> —Alonso

Alonso's entire family, including the children, worked as migrant workers when he was growing up. Although his father started the family's farm in eastern Washington in the 1970s, Alonso continued to work for other people to make extra money until he was an adult himself and could live out his dream of operating his own farm full time. He recalled to me the experiences of his father, one of the first Mexican farmers in their region, over forty years ago:

> You know, down at the warehouse selling your own produce and getting a decent grade ... because it felt, and my father also felt, that when they take a box of asparagus and grab like eight ounces, they pick it up and put it on the table. They grade that and they knock a whole percentage off the total of your weight, five hundred or six hundred pounds, or wherever you got. And my dad always felt that he wasn't getting a fair grading like everybody else. So that became an issue for a long time. And then he would go in to make sure. ... My dad took the time to almost grade every box, and he still didn't get a good grade. So he was like, "That's bullshit, we are getting rigged."

Although he and his father before him are some of the few Mexican immigrants who have been successful in starting their own farms, Alonso still recognizes the deep-seated resentment many white farmers have against his family. For people of color, transitioning to a new position in the agrarian class hierarchy is not without struggle in the United States. This is largely due to the historical commitment of farmers and others with decision-making powers to maintain people of color in working-class positions.

In this chapter, I tie together the histories of slavery and immigration as they relate to US agrarian labor politics in order to unpack the challenges faced by Mexican American farmers in the United States today. Through a historical analysis of the relationship between race, labor, and land access in the United States, we begin to see why people of color, and Mexican immigrants in particular, struggle to advance on the so-called agricultural ladder. The ladder metaphor has come to represent agricultural opportunity for class advancement in the context of an idealized Jeffersonian or private land ethic. It is only by situating this model within the framework of race relations that the true and unequal nature of agrarian development in the United States becomes clear.

The United States has a long history of constituting full citizenship, and related rights to land and resources, through whiteness. The earliest colonists utilized social constructions of race to justify the taking of native lands and exploitation of native labor in the founding as well as expansion of the nation. The labor to establish the agrarian landscape was maintained by African slaves, who were taken from their own lands to work on US soil, followed by the work of their children and grandchildren. Once freed, African Americans were systematically denied full rights to land, mobility, and participation in the democratic process.

Since emancipation, slave descendants and immigrants have composed the majority of the agrarian labor force. Legislation and cultural exclusions have been designed to maintain a steady and available agrarian workforce composed of people of color. Immigrants and blacks have been excluded from full citizenship rights in the United States due to state-sanctioned policies, which have been reinforced by everyday experiences of racial exclusion. Those who have attempted to access their own land to farm, including nonwhite immigrant farmers, have been dispossessed of land and resources, explicitly due to their racial and citizenship status (Chan 1989; Foley 1999; Minkoff-Zern et al. 2011; Matsumoto 1993; Wells 1991, 1996).

The challenges faced by Mexican immigrants in starting their own farm operations in the United States today are intimately tied to the agrarian history of both the United States and Mexico, and the ways in which specific classes of people have been racialized, and therefore marginalized in gaining access to land and capital over time. Farmers and landowners have historically taken advantage of Mexican immigrants' politically vulnerable citizenship status in particular, be it as documented temporary workers, undocumented workers, or even documented workers with relationships in the undocumented worker community, to deny workers human rights and a living wage (Garcia 2002; Mitchell 1996; Hahamovitch 1997; Barndt 2008).

I begin this chapter by discussing the flaws in the agricultural ladder metaphor as it intersects with an understanding of racial exclusion and discrimination in the United States. I then look at the African American experience of slave labor, sharecropping, and farm ownership as historical context for the Mexican immigrant struggle in agriculture today. I argue that black Americans were forced to stay at the lowest rungs of the ladder due to discriminatory policies and day-to-day racism. In the next section, I examine the condition of Mexican exceptionalism: how farmers and policy makers *racism* have produced an image of Mexican immigrants as temporary workers, in effect preventing them from advancing up the agricultural ladder as they are systematically blocked from establishing themselves as citizens and farmers in this country. Finally, I conclude with an analysis of the US agricultural census, and how this measure of participation in agriculture in the United States today provides glimpses of hope for immigrant advancement as well as a view into the problematic ways immigrant farmers are undercounted and overlooked.

Race and the Agricultural Ladder

The agricultural ladder is a metaphor and model used by agricultural economists, rural sociologists, and others to describe the rate and means by which unpaid farmhands and hired farmworkers have advanced to positions as farm owner-operators, particularly in the United States (see, for example, Spillman 1919; Lee 1947; Kloppenburg and Geisler 1985). Although it was widely applied, especially in the first half of the twentieth century, this theoretical model has also been critiqued for lacking empirical rigor and accuracy (Kloppenburg and Geisler 1985).

The idea of the agricultural ladder is rooted in the "agrarian myth" or "agrarian imaginary," which promotes the notion that in the United States, a country founded by hardworking individual farmers, land access has been democratically distributed. Jack Kloppenburg and Charles Geisler (1985) argue that it is ultimately more useful when seen as an ideological model, promoting the idealized image of the small-scale US farmer. The ladder concept reinforces the idea that all individuals who work the land diligently with their own hands (with no help from slave or hired labor) have access to upward agrarian mobility.

This kind of agrarian idealism could not be further from the truth. Land-ownership was originally obtained through the pilfering of native lands. While the narrative is often espoused that land cultivated by white settlers in the United States was previously "untouched," native lands throughout the Americas were utilized for agriculture, grazing, and other livelihood practices. Indigenous practices were in some cases even more intensive and productive than those of white farmers, yet they were not recognized as such. Native farmers and ranchers were not seen as viable agriculturalists as their practices did not produce goods for capitalist accumulation, and thus they were forced via violent means from the lands that they occupied (Buck 2001; Mann 2005).

Rather than a country built on an ethic of the democratic distribution of land, access to land, capital, and other resources to build productive agricultural businesses has been monopolized into the hands of fewer and fewer farm owner-operators since the end of the nineteenth century. This concentration of land and agrarian wealth correlates with the increased mechanization and industrialization of agriculture, and related pressure and competition to scale up operations (Buttel and Flinn 1975; Guthman 2014; Kloppenburg and Geisler 1985; Walker 2004). When one starts to account for racialized disparities in land access and owner occupancy throughout US history, the story becomes even more disproportionate.

Despite valid critiques, the agricultural ladder has been continuously used as a way to understand and justify agrarian mobility in the United States, and through this lens, minimize the focus on unequal power relations. The traditional use of the agrarian ladder model in US academic discourse recognizes the advantages of inherited access to land and other resources as well as differing access to capital among social classes, and the importance of social status within differing historical and political contexts (Lee 1947). Yet until more recent discussion by historians, social mobility in agriculture, or ascent up the ladder, has been written about as a concept hinged on hard work and tenacity, absent of a racial or gendered analysis.

In the US-based literature, it is implicitly assumed that the farmworker or potential farmer is both white and male.[1]

The denial of race in more traditional discussions of agricultural economic and class ascendance has functioned to reinforce rationalizations in academic and policy-based settings of people of color as stagnant laborers in the US agricultural system (for a broader exploration of race-based challenges for immigrant farmers, see chapter 3). Further, as I argue below, such framings justify the poor treatment of racialized agricultural workers as they are portrayed as unable or unworthy of the responsibilities of becoming farm owner-operators. The historical racial divide in reference to access to land, capital, and other resources is reflective of a deeply ingrained agrarian culture that privileges the white majority. This culture has been normalized and institutionalized, ensuring a racialized landscape of land-ownership and business ownership.

Slavery, Sharecropping, and Black Ascendance Up the Ladder

To understand racialized differences with regard to land and agrarian opportunity, one must lay the groundwork by first looking at the experience of black Americans and slavery, and how this history has continued to impact their ability to farm independently. Following emancipation, many were given hope that they would finally achieve the status of landed citizen and the freedom of owning their own farm business. Unfortunately those dreams were mostly unrealized. In order to maintain access to free and available black labor, white landowners created social and institutional barriers to prevent freed slaves from accessing land. These barriers created challenges to land access for black, aspiring farmers for decades.

After Emancipation

African American farmers in the United States, like immigrant farmers of color, have been displaced from their livelihoods many times over. They were first dispossessed through the processes of capture from their homelands. As slaves, they could not legally own property, although they could acquire capital. On emancipation in 1865, slaves were promised "forty acres and a mule." This refers to a statement made by Clinton B. Fisk, a senior officer in the federal Freedman's Bureau during Reconstruction, who contributed to a vision of black yeomanry held by many slaves themselves. Fisk and others claimed that freed slaves would benefit from widespread land reform following the Civil War as reparations for generations of unpaid labor. Yet land that had been claimed during the Civil War was mostly returned to its white owners rather than being redistributed to the black slaves who had worked it, as had been pledged (Cox 1958; McKenzie 1993; Williamson 1965).[2] Politicians in both the North and South perceived black landownership as a threat, as white landowners and other business owners saw available black labor as essential for economic productivity. In many southern states, "Black Codes" were developed specifically targeting freed slaves, including laws denying black people the right to own property or lease land, and restricting mobility. These laws were designed to maintain a restricted black workforce, which would reflect the labor system of slavery as much as possible (Cohen 1991; Flynn 1999; McKenzie 1993).

In addition to these legal restrictions in many states, after emancipation the majority of freed slaves lacked the capital or land to become true tenants or landowners. Most stayed in agriculture as laborers or sharecroppers. Sharecroppers, both black and white, farmed a specific plot of land as permitted by the landowner, in most cases with seeds, fertilizers, and other inputs provided, and using farming methods as dictated by the landowner, in exchange for a percentage of the crop as income. This was a step above their former position as a slave or wage laborer, but a far cry from having control over one's land and labor, or being a true tenant of the land. This position on the ladder typically only existed in the South as a direct extension of slaveholding agrarian culture (Alston and Kauffman 1998).

Over time, a small portion of black sharecroppers ascended to the position of a "true tenant," paying rent either in the form of a set number of crops or cash. Yet once they became tenant farmers, they had a much smaller chance to advance to landownership than their white tenant counterparts. Structural and individual cases of overt racism kept many black tenants from even trying to access their own land (Stine 1990). In addition to lacking access to capital and resources to purchase land and farming inputs, after emancipation there was a mass migration of black people from the rural South to cities as well as northern and western states in search of nonagrarian lives, and different opportunities for work and community.

It is also important to note that the number of black farmers who worked as sharecroppers versus those who rented land as actual share or cash tenants is hard to decipher in the period after emancipation as the US agricultural census did not distinguish between the two until after 1920 (Alston and Kauffman 1998). Some historians argue that the number of true tenants and black farm operators (versus sharecroppers) during this time was actually much higher than the census reveals (McKenzie 1993).

Notwithstanding sharecropping as the norm, among those who stayed in agriculture, some black tenants eventually saved enough capital to purchase their own land. By the end of the nineteenth century, 25 percent of black farm operators in the United States owned the land that they farmed (Alston and Kauffman 1998). Despite disadvantages in accessing land, former black slaves and later wage laborers, similar to the immigrant farmworkers of today, had experience farming, gardening, and marketing for their employers, giving them an agricultural knowledge base from which to draw when attempting to go out on their own and start commercial farms. In particular areas, especially in the cotton and rice-growing regions of the deep South, former slaves were especially successful by creatively accessing land at lower rates if their owners had not paid taxes during the war or by collectively pooling resources to purchase land (Van Sant 2016).

Civil Rights Era

After a short-lived increase in black farm ownership from 1900 through 1920, however, when black-owned farms reached their height of 925,000, a steady decline began in black farm business ownership and land tenure.[3] This decrease has been attributed to overt threats of racial violence and discrimination, rising urban job opportunities, and increasing mechanization. Since black farmers had less access to either capital to invest in new machinery or the larger plots of land necessary to compete in an increasingly industrialized agriculture system than did their white counterparts, they were not able to maintain a competitive level of production. Additionally, black farmers have been squeezed out by the state, experiencing overtly racist treatment at USDA offices and differential opportunities than those offered to their white counterparts. These inequalities were partially addressed in 1999 by the class action lawsuits *Pigford v. Glickman* and *Brewington v. Glickman* (Daniel 2013; Gilbert, Sharp and Felin 2002; Grim 1996; Payne 1991; Ponder 1971; Schweninger 1989; Simon 1993; Van Sant 2016).[4]

In addition to racial biases as well as economic and cultural boundaries to class ascendance, black farmers posed a challenge to white landowners as their advancement up the ladder signified the loss of a dependable pool of cheap labor. Despite white farmers' attempts to maintain this labor force, black agricultural workers eventually migrated out of the rural South for industrial and urban jobs in bigger, more northern cities. They were largely replaced by Mexican and other Latin American immigrant workers, brought in through explicit international labor agreements and manufactured immigrant streams, as I will discuss in the next section.

Black agriculturalists' largely unsuccessful transition from slave to land-owner and farm operator set the racialized backdrop for a mostly Mexican workforce to replace them, and to eventually contend with similar challenges around their racialized agrarian class positioning. The institutional challenges for black farmers to ascend the agricultural ladder created a cultural and institutional norm in which farmers in the United States are normalized as white, and workers are normalized as people of color. The limitations black farmers have faced over time reinforce an environment where Mexicans and other nonwhite immigrant workers and aspiring farmers struggle to advance economically and culturally in US agriculture.

Mexican Exceptionalism: The Creation of a Racialized, Temporary Workforce

Mexican immigrants, much like former slaves and their descendants, have faced race-related challenges to advancing up the so-called agricultural ladder. Analogous to black agricultural laborers, they have had to contend with being politically and culturally categorized as workers rather than owners in the US agrarian laborer-to-owner hierarchy. This institutionalized hierarchy has systematically benefited white landowners and business owners. For the most part, white farmers have successfully maintained Mexican immigrants' working class position in rural areas, laboring and living in a continuous state of poverty. US industrial growers have consistently benefited from policies that enable them to employ and underpay Mexican-born workers, while ensuring they are denied the same rights and opportunities for upward mobility as US-born white workers. In this section, I discuss some of the moments in US-Mexican relations that have broadly established the conditions Mexican immigrant farmers endure today.

The exact boundaries of the US-Mexican border were contested for many years, particularly along the US-Texas perimeter—a dispute that led to the

Mexican-American War of 1846–1848. For people native to the Americas, on both sides of the political boundary, the border literally crossed them, as the saying goes. Most, if not all, Mexican immigrants whom I interviewed are of some part native heritage, with some identifying specifically as indigenous. The fact that they have been identified as native to one country yet as illegal or foreign in another, based on a politically defined boundary with little relevance to their actual ancestry, is an irony not lost on them.

Conversely, many people born in Mexico are light skinned and often claim to be of Spanish/European lineage, identifying as white themselves. Yet Mexicans have long been recognized as nonwhite by US white-identifying citizens, no matter the color of their skin, as a way to differentiate and categorize them as lower status in the intersecting US racial and class hierarchies. As Neal Foley's (1999) work on agrarian class hierarchies in early twentieth-century Texas shows, Mexicans were seen as a clear economic and cultural threat to US-born whites, and racialized as closer equals to blacks than whites. This racialization provided a justification for landowners to limit Mexican workers' and sharecroppers' available credit and autonomy, therefore restricting their ability to ascend to tenant or landowner status.

Although Mexican immigrants have been categorized as nonwhite, it has also been argued that they are different than other racialized groups of immigrant workers to the United States, as I discuss below. In order to preserve their worker status and prevent them from accessing land, politicians and farmers have invoked the geographic proximity of Mexico to make a case that unlike other immigrants to the United States, they are able and wish to return to their home country rather than establish a life in the US. It has been claimed that Mexican immigrants do not pose the same risk as other immigrants to the economy and "American" rural culture, because at the end of the season they will return to their home country and communities. This argument has been used to further justify the qualification of Mexican immigrants as workers only. As a racialized and immigrant agrarian workforce, they do not qualify for the same rights as US-born workers, and certainly are not afforded equal access to land and other resources. Their categorization as temporary laborers further complicates their challenges in being accepted into rural communities as landowners and permanent residents.

To understand the state of Mexican farmers and agricultural workers in the United States today, we must return to history for context. In the sections that follow, I outline the policies that have produced an image of Mexican immigrant workers as both necessary and illegal. What becomes clear through this historical analysis are the ways that Mexican workers have been framed as exceptional from other immigrants in their impermanence in the United States, and therefore not lasting or ascending on the agricultural ladder of class advancement.

World War I Era

The case of Mexican immigrants' exceptionalism begins during World War I, a time period during which Mexican immigrants were prioritized over others seeking to migrate to the US, given that their stay would only be temporary. Mexicans and other Latin Americans were singled out from other immigrants in 1917, when the first comprehensive immigration law in the United States was passed by Congress. Congress passed this act in the context of the war as a means to restrict anyone who was perceived as a threat to US security. In addition to instating a literacy test and raising the "head tax," the price of the tax paid by new immigrants, the act restricted immigration by anyone from the "Asiatic Barred Zone." The zone included any person from a country that was on or adjacent to Asia but was "not owned by the U.S.," with the exception of Japanese and Filipinos (Tucker and Creller 2007). This act provided no restrictions on immigrants from the rest of the Americas, and in the midst of this new anti-immigrant legislation, the US Department of Labor directed an order to bring in temporary Mexican workers and families for six months, without them having to pay head taxes or passing literary clauses. Despite a growing culture of xenophobia in the United States at the time, Mexican workers were prioritized for entry, while other immigrants' admittance was being limited.

In 1924, a new immigration bill was passed, and it included the National Origins Act as well as the Asian Exclusions Act. This federal law restricted the number of immigrants who could be admitted to the United States to 2 percent of the number of people from that country who were already living in the United States as of the 1890 census, and was specifically designed to target southern and eastern Europeans, particularly Italian and Jewish immigrants. Additionally, it severely limited the immigration of Africans, and outright banned the immigration of Asians and Arabs. According to the US Department of State, Office of the Historian (2017), the purpose of the act was "to preserve the ideal of American homogeneity." Moreover, in the early twentieth century, a series of acts called the Alien Land Laws were passed in over a dozen states. The main purpose of these laws was to exclude Asian immigrants from holding land as well as force practicing farmers off land that they were already cultivating (Matsumoto 1993).

The National Origins Act sparked a massive debate between hard-line immigration restrictionists, who argued for more class- and citizenship-based immigration limitations, and antirestrictionists, who did not want to see immigration further limited. Antirestrictionists included those who benefited from immigrant labor, such as cotton growers, ranchers, and farmers. Historian Kathleen Mapes has shown the ways that these agriculturalists intervened in congressional hearings regarding Mexican labor specifically. Farmers argued that Mexican workers were a "special class of labor" that would never settle permanently, and "could be called in and exported at will" (Mapes 2004, 68). Mapes analyzes the testimony of midwestern sugar beet farmers who contended that Mexican workers were not only *not* a threat as permanent community residents but furthermore would never succeed at challenging the racial hierarchy of US farming as they knew it—they simply were not skilled enough to start farms on their own. She writes, "To address fears that once in rural areas Mexicans might climb the agricultural ladder, some Midwestern witnesses insisted that though Mexicans were especially suited for unskilled farm labor, they would never compete with skilled farm laborers or attempt to buy land and begin farming on their own. As evidence, a farmer from Minnesota, F. H. Ross, told Congress, 'I do not believe that there is any Mexican who is ever going to own a farm'" (ibid., 7).

The justification for continuing to allow Mexican workers entry to the country was further supported by farmers who believed that not only were Mexicans naturally "unskilled" but also that the future of white family farming in the United States depended on their racialized labor.

> The flip side of this "new world" of agriculture was that Mexican workers would have no "agricultural ladder." Sugar industrialists and farmers justified the lack of opportunity for the newest agricultural workers by turning to racist assumptions. Since Mexicans as a "race" were already "degraded," employing them to work in the fields where opportunities for advancement were few, and mobility was always physical and not financial, did not contradict the Jeffersonian ideal but made it possible in a new world of industrial agriculture. (ibid., 10)

This argument reflects the case made by white landowners during the period after emancipation regarding limiting prospects for black workers and sharecroppers. Agricultural employers believed that denying workers of color opportunities for advancement was a necessary condition for maintaining white family farming as they knew it. The antirestrictionists ultimately won, and Latin American immigration was not limited by the act. Mexican immigrants continued to cross the border, filling labor gaps on US farms.

Immigration debates throughout the last century have perpetuated the notion that Mexican immigrants do not wish to stay in the United States, particularly as such debates have intersected with policies regarding agricultural labor. As Mapes (ibid., 72) observes, "The argument that Mexicans would not assimilate or adopt U.S. citizenship was developed into a racist theory that Mexicans were naturally drawn back to Mexico." Ensuring a racialized and easily controlled workforce for industrial agriculture became a consistently invoked assertion for allowing Mexicans entry to the United States, without extending an option for citizenship and related rights.

Bracero Era

The policy of allowing entry but restricting permanent residence was institutionalized in the 1940s through the Bracero Program. In order to guarantee an agrarian workforce from Mexico, the Bracero Program was established through a set of accords between the United States and Mexico in 1942. The program allowed Mexican workers to legally cross the border to work in US agribusiness on a temporary basis. This diplomatic agreement was developed to address the labor shortages created by World War II on the US side, and deep-seated poverty on the Mexican side. This policy solidified the patterns of migration that have continued from Mexico to the United States, both legally and illegally, ever since.

More than two million Mexican workers came to labor in the United States as part of the Bracero Program, until it was eliminated in 1964. Specific employers contracted workers to do a particular job as part of the agreement. There was no opportunity for changing jobs if the workers was unsatisfied, abused, or found the job expectations unreasonable. The Mexican government paid workers, but only once they completed their contract and returned home. Costs, such as transportation, housing, and food, were deducted from their pay. Some growers tricked workers out of their pay, telling them they could stay longer and then reporting employees to deportation authorities so they didn't have to pay the workers at the end of the season. Bracero workers were regularly denied their full pay on return. Eventually, in 2007, the Mexican government offered "cash assistance" payments of $3,700 to former braceros, who for decades had claimed payment fraud. Of course, by then few workers could be tracked down, and many were no longer alive (Mitchell 2012; Mize and Swords 2010).

As the program continued past the wartime era of labor shortage, braceros were strategically used to undercut wages and rights demanded by domestically born workers. This created a tension in which many US-born workers and union organizers saw braceros as a threat to their livelihoods and organizing abilities. Ultimately, the presence of the braceros over the course of more than two decades helped shape the economic and cultural structures of US agriculture, especially in the highly industrial fields of California. These structures have created an economic expectation that growers should be able to underpay and exploit the labor of workers. Further, it created a cultural expectation that because those workers are foreign-born and racialized Mexicans, they do not need to be paid or treated as well as US citizens, and should be grateful for the work (Mitchell 2012). This historical tension underpins much of the negativity targeted at Mexican immigrants by economically disempowered and underemployed US citizens today, despite the fact that domestic workers have shown that they will not take available jobs in agricultural labor, given the current wages and conditions (Clemens 2013; Powell 2012).

Yet even in the midst of this massive binational labor agreement, some in the United States were already waging war against "illegal" Mexicans, who they did not want to see enter the United States under any circumstances. In many states, including Texas, Colorado, Illinois, Indiana, Michigan, Montana, Minnesota, Wisconsin, and Wyoming, the anti-Mexican sentiment and sanctioned discrimination was so strong, in fact, that the Mexican government prevented braceros from working in those states for the first several years of the agreement. The government was concerned that the workers would not be protected from racially discriminatory practices.

Anti-Mexican sentiment grew alongside the constant industry demand for cheap immigrant labor, with this contradiction entrenching itself in the fabric of rural areas. In 1954, the first federal program designed to explicitly target and deport Mexican immigrants was put into place. During Operation

Wetback (the official name), the Immigration and Naturalization Service actively deported 1.3 million people, mostly undocumented, but also some legal temporary workers as well as US citizens of Mexican descent.[5] Most of these immigrants had followed the migrant streams established through the Bracero Program, which was running at its peak during the course of this mass repatriation project (Mize and Swords 2010).

Operation Wetback was the first massive drive to actively deport undocumented and even documented Mexicans from the United States. It was also the first time that a public relations campaign was used to target Mexicans, branding them as "illegal." The US attorney general at the time, Howard Brownell, and a former lieutenant general, Joseph Swing, hired to run the project, constructed a mass media campaign, sending out regular press releases, and controlling media coverage regarding the success of the deportations and messages supporting the Immigration and Naturalization Service's motives. The creation of a divide between US-born citizens and Mexican immigrants as well as those of Mexican descent has persisted to this day in political discourse and media coverage of immigration debates, constructing a narrative of Mexican people in the United States as illegal, and less deserving of rights to citizenship, land, and class mobility (Bacon 2008; Mize and Swords 2010).

Additionally, Operation Wetback was the first call to militarize the US-Mexican border, which the attorney general labeled as out of control, employing military professionals to manage the situation. Many of the current border control practices were established during this time, such as regular sweeps and roundups of found crossers using military equipment, orchestrated by the US Border Patrol and local officials. It was during this period that the construction of a "wall," or chain-link fence, along parts of the border was first proposed (Mize and Swords 2010). The militarization of the border has, of course, continued too, and the construction of a wall along the border has been one of the most contentious issues of Trump's presidential campaign and administration.

Post-Bracero Era

Although the Bracero Program ended in 1964, Mexican workers have continued to dominate the US agricultural industry, albeit with little increase in worker protections or rights, and in an increasingly hostile environment to immigrants. They have remained a vulnerable workforce, both as a largely undocumented immigrant population and group of workers excepted from labor laws. These economic and cultural challenges have led to a stagnant position on the ladder to farm ownership for most Mexican agricultural workers today.

From the end of the Bracero Program until the 1980s, little was done to legally address the regular hiring of undocumented workers in agriculture. Then, in 1986, President Ronald Reagan signed the IRCA, which followed the contradictory tradition in the United States of both abetting the structural conditions encouraging low-paid immigrant labor and criminalizing the people who perform it. On the one hand, the IRCA designated a 50 percent increase in border control and made it explicitly illegal for employers to knowingly employ undocumented workers, and therefore effectively made it illegal for those workers to be employed. On the other hand, the act gave amnesty to over one million "Special Agricultural Workers"—people who could prove they had worked in the United States for over sixty days between May 1985 and May 1986. For the first time, the IRCA made it an explicit crime to be hired in the United States without legal citizenship or working papers. Following this notion of the necessary yet illegal worker, the US government sent Mexican immigrants the message, "We don't want you to cross the border illegally, but we know you are here, and if you already work here, you can stay." While creating contradictory policy for agricultural workers, it did nothing to address the long-established patterns of migration from Mexican to US fields, or the economically dependent relationship that US policy had historically created.

Given both the perception of Mexican immigrants as somehow different from other workers and their dominance in agricultural labor in the United States, it is somewhat unsurprising that the laws to protect them are also exceptional from other labor laws and protections. Farm labor is one of few occupations exempt from the federal Fair Labor Standards Act of 1938, which established a minimum wage, forty-hour workweek, and overtime pay, and prohibited child labor. Farmworkers are not included in most state minimum wage and work hours limitations, with the exceptions of California, Oregon, and Washington. Farmworkers were also excluded from the National Labor Relations Act of 1935, which guarantees the rights of private sector employees to join a union and engage in collective bargaining. This is with the exception of California and, very recently, New York. In California, farmworkers fought for and won that right in 1975 after a prolonged effort by the United Farm Workers. They are now covered under the California Agricultural Labor Relations Act. In New York, a dairy worker, Crispin Hernandez, recently filed and won a lawsuit arguing that by being denied the right to organize and collectively bargain, farmworkers were being denied rights guaranteed by the state's constitution. Yet even when laws do exist to protect workers, research has shown that they are routinely ignored by employers and not enforced by relevant authorities (Gray 2013). As a racialized and hidden workforce, farm labor has been structurally stripped of the same rights as other workers in the United States.

Anthropologist Seth Holmes, in his in-depth ethnographic study with Mixtec and Triqui immigrants, discusses the interrelated ethnic and labor hierarchies that exist on family owned berry farms in the Skagit Valley of Washington, one of the regions I also researched for this book. He depicts multiple layers of farm hierarchies, with third-generation Japanese immigrant farm owners and white farm executives at the top, and indigenous berry pickers at the bottom. Farm structures and policies as well as economic, linguistic, and cultural divides all function to segregate owners, administrators, crop managers, field supervisors, and checkers, who are mostly white, and US-born Latino/as from undocumented indigenous immigrants, who do the majority of the hard labor and live in poverty conditions on the farm. These social and economic divisions reinforce the notion that the smaller-statured and darker-skinned indigenous immigrants are less "civilized," and not worthy of respect or career advancement (Holmes 2013). These segregations and conditions are common on US farms, as studies of farm labor across regions can account for (Fox et al. 2017; Hahamovitch 1997; Mares 2019; Mines, Nichols, and Runsten 2010; Minkoff-Zern 2014a, 2014b). Such ethnic and citizenship-based divisions also cement workers in their underpaid status on farms, preventing them from advancing to the role of farm owner.

Rather than support increases to wages that would make agricultural labor a desirable profession for domestically born workers, the agricultural lobby and politicians in rural regions of the country continue to fight for increases in guest worker programs. The H2A seasonal worker visa program is specifically for agricultural workers, continuing a Bracero era approach to limiting workers to a particular employer for a restricted period of time. Similar to the bracero laborers, as visiting workers, they have no right to change jobs and labor organizing is nearly unheard of. The agricultural lobby continually reasserts the H2A program as a win-win situation for farmers and workers alike, alluding to the condescending argument that Mexicans only want to come to the United States to work and then prefer to go home. This justification for temporary and guest worker programs is being endorsed heavily by industry today, as it feels vulnerable under a presidential administration that is overtly hostile to the Mexican immigrants on whom it depends.[6]

Through this political process of simultaneously bringing in and also forcefully deporting workers, Mexican immigrants have been constructed as illegal, removable, and ultimately temporary. Rather than seen as the backbone of US agriculture and the potential hope for the continuance of family farming, Mexican immigrants have been constantly held back as they struggle to obtain the right to work and live in the United States, attempting to become embedded into agrarian communities and cultures. The construction of Mexican immigrants as illegal and forever foreign, while also economically necessary as laborers, creates a condition in which their ascendance up the agricultural ladder is fraught with structural racial discrimination and economic hardship. Yet as this book shows, many have fought against these incredible odds to make their vision a reality. In the section below, I look to census data to understand where and in what kinds of agriculture Latino/as, as a broader group of farmers, are succeeding, focusing on the ways that many immigrant farmers are being left out of official counts.

The Agricultural Census and the Missing Numbers

The US Census of Agriculture is administered by the National Agricultural Statistics Service (NASS) of the USDA every five years, with the goal of recording all farms and ranches in the United States. Based on this reporting, farm groups lobby for money and other resources, agricultural policies are determined, and rural priorities are established. According to the census, while the majority of US farm ownership remains white, Latino/a farmers are rising in the ranks of farm ownership and operation on a national scale. Among farmers who identify as being of "Spanish, Latino, or Hispanic" origin, there was a 21 percent increase between 2007 and 2012 among principal farm operators. In contrast, the principal operators of the total number of farms, Latino/a farmers included, declined 4 percent over this time period.[7]

Additionally, and in concurrence with my own qualitative research, the census shows that Latino/a-operated farms are disproportionately smaller in acreage and lower in sales than other farms. Fifty-eight percent of Hispanic farms were smaller than fifty acres, as compared to 39 percent of the total farms. Their land is also more likely to be rented. Further, they are more likely to not have internet access and work at least part time at an off-farm job (USDA 2014).

In states where Latino/a farmers have a larger recorded presence, such as California and Washington (and therefore are easier to draw conclusions about via census data), they disproportionately cultivated vegetables and melons, fruit and nut trees, flowers, and plant starts (greenhouse/nursery), as compared with animals, grains, tobacco, cotton, or sugar (ibid.). The census does not distinguish between immigrants and nonimmigrants, so these numbers do not reflect my own research population precisely. Yet the census is the only comprehensive data comparing farmers across all states and regions, and can demonstrate trends in growing practices for context. As I discuss below, my more concentrated regional and interview-based research shows that most immigrant Latino/a farmers do not answer the agricultural census survey, leaving gaps in our knowledge concerning their population numbers and growing practices.

Although the census shows an undeniable growth in Latino/Hispanic farmers, I argue that Latino/a immigrants are generally being undercounted in these numbers, and nonwhite Latino/as (indigenous or mestizo) are not being counted at all. The census is a self-reported questionnaire, and although it is required by law that farmers respond, there is no enforcement, so many who receive the questionnaire by mail simply ignore it. In immigrant farmers' cases, this could be due to a lack of literacy or English-language skills, or aversion to filling out government documents for fear of being deported.

Most farmers are initially identified by NASS through landownership or rental agreements. They are also identified through previous contact with the USDA if they have applied for loans, insurance, or received other kinds of support. Additionally, other agrarian institutions such as university extension services, nonprofit organizations, and farmers markets may share farmer contact info with NASS to help it find growers. There is also follow-up by census staff members to check on accuracy, and they supplement self-reporting with a land-based survey. NASS employees double check numbers by knocking on doors and doing interviews.

The off-the-grid approach that many immigrant farmers take to farming makes it difficult for census staff to identify and count these farmers. Almost none of the farmers I interviewed had ever heard of the agricultural census. They farm on mostly rented land, often under informal agreements, and rarely live on the farm or have paperwork documenting their land rental agreements. Even those who do own their land, usually do not live on the same property where they farm. In my discussions with staff members at NASS, university extension services, and the USDA, who all do some level of outreach to Hispanic/Latino populations for the survey, they confirmed that they have increased outreach to all farming groups deemed as "socially disadvantaged" in recent years. Yet they also agreed that the farmers discussed in this study are still underrepresented in the census.

In my conversation with Christopher Mertz, the director of the NASS Northwest Regional Field Office, he told me that he was aware of Spanish-speaking staff involved in the data collection process in New Mexico and Washington. He mentioned that there could be Spanish-speaking staff in other states as well, but could not confirm it. The presence of Spanish-speaking staff was usually the result of farming organizations in these regions actively seeking more resources for Latino/a farmers. He added that even despite this additional outreach, "We get plenty of feedback that they are undercounting certain populations. Definitely, we don't get them all. It's a sample."

Mertz explained the process of collecting farmer data and challenges of getting farmers counted who are out of the USDA's general networks. In the northwest region, NASS reaches out to organizations that work with nontraditional farmers more directly. Of course, these organizations must exist for NASS to access their networks, so in regions where no such organization is present, the problem is even greater. As Mertz observes,

> It is a challenge to capture [their numbers in the census] if they don't work with farm programs and are not part of farm organizations. We work with organizations that do work with them, like Viva Farms. We were looking at the names of the farmers they work with, and the plan for next census is to work with them. ... Sometimes we have problems because organizations don't want to give the names of farmers. ... We try to find names and sources any way we can. We try to account for farm incubators as well. We are always developing our lists.

He noted that it is especially difficult to count farmers who rent land using informal arrangements: "That acreage is accounted for by the farm owner." He added that in his region, he believes the numbers are becoming increasingly more accurate, yet it is still hard to know who they are missing, adding, "I think we are doing a better job of counting and finding these people. … But some people enter agriculture and leave before we can ever count them."

Robert, a staff member who works in the USDA's FSA office in the Hudson Valley region of New York, explained his office's role in census outreach:

Figure 2.1
Sabino Flores of Flores Farm with Kate Selting Smith, who works with Viva Farms as part of the Northwest Small and Latino Farm Support Program at Washington State University's School of Environment and Skagit County Extension.

"We get the pamphlets. ... If you don't come in, you're not going to see that then. Sometimes even our guys who are getting a call about it might not answer or take the time to really do it. ... Even our traditional farmers don't respond to it."

When I asked directly about the census including Latino/a farmers, he stated that to his knowledge, "very, very little" of them were counted. As I found in my interviews with immigrant farmers themselves, as Robert assumes, most would never have heard of it.

Marcy Ostrom directs the Small Farm Program for Washington State University, housed in the Center for Sustaining Natural Resources. She has committed much of her career to researching the needs of small-scale Latino/a farmers in her region, and finding the best ways to outreach and address their problems as small farmers.[8] In discussing her extension work with Latino/a farmers in her region, she explained how her staff got involved with agricultural census data collection outreach:

> The ag census was not showing any or very few [Latino/a farmers], and I was with [a colleague] who kept saying that they had a list of 150 Latino-owned small farms. I went to my extension chair and said, 'Do you know any of these farms?' And they said no. So it is a bigger problem than the Latino farms. It's about small farms. So that's how I started getting involved in this. They were invisible, and people who went to look for them started going to churches and soccer fields, and giving trainings for farmworkers and asking how many people have their own farm. This was in 2005. He showed me a list of 250 Latino-owned farms. ... I actually sent his list to the agricultural census, and they hired him as a numerator, so it got better. It was still missing a lot.

Additionally, as I discuss in more depth in chapter 3, given their histories of immigration and relationship to US government agencies, many immigrant farmers are resistant to fill out government paperwork. When I asked Mertz, from NASS, about the reluctance of certain groups of farmers, especially immigrants, to fill out paperwork, he confirmed their hesitancy: "We get that from every segment of the ag population, especially if they are undocumented. By law we can't share individual information even to other USDA agencies. ... Our confidentiality rules have been around forever. There's a lot of education to that. Many people are unaware that this research helps [them access resources]." While Mertz notes that the confidentiality of responses is bound by law, it is difficult for immigrants to trust a government agency, particularly in a moment when they have been so vilified by the US presidential administration. Further, he notes that the benefits of the census are largely unknown to immigrant communities.

To further complicate how immigrants might be counted by the census, should they choose to respond, Hispanic/Latino is considered an ethnicity, not a race, by the survey. If they check to be identified as of "Spanish, Latino, or Hispanic" origin, they must also choose a "race," which includes the options American Indian or Alaska native, Asian, black or African American, native Hawaiian or Pacific Islander, or white. None of these are representative of the farmers I interviewed, who are mostly brown skinned. Although almost all are of at least partial native Mexican descent, they do not identify with the term "American Indian." Mertz, at the census, agreed that the options for ethnic and racial identification are flawed: "Yes, it's difficult [the ethnicity/ race question]. Some answer 'other' or just don't finish filling it out. It's not really great. They don't answer it how it's supposed to be. I typically don't give them advice. Someone might not answer that entire question. We will try to pull previously reported information to fill in missing data. ... We can't change that category; it comes from a higher level of government."

Despite these issues, the census is still the only comprehensive national agricultural data that exists, and provides context for racial and ethnic shifts occurring in US agriculture. Additionally, the census is incredibly important for farmers, especially those who are economically and socially disadvantaged, in order to gain access to resources. As Mertz notes, "These numbers help organizations get funding for their programs. The Center for Latino Farmers go to DC and ask for more funding based on high Latino farmers numbers via the census."

It's pertinent that Latino/a farmers' existence is properly accounted for, as the census is crucial to resource access. Resources such as targeted non-profit support, outreach, and grants can only be specified for immigrant and other Latino/a farmers from the federal and state government if they are counted. Yet as I describe above, my interviews showed that many of the most vulnerable farmers are not accounted for in this survey. This is one more way that the agricultural ladder functionally leaves immigrants and other farmers of color off its top rungs, as they are not seen and provided for as part of the nation's farm-operating class.

Conclusion

Levi Van Sant (2016, 197) aptly explains these uneven rural histories through the notion of plantation geographies, or "the regional reproduction of racial hierarchy through the white monopolization of land and attendant claims to agrarian citizenship. The resulting social formation is shaped by improvement projects that firmly articulate whiteness (understood as a normative and unexamined racial identity) and agricultural governance." These processes have succeeded in creating regionalized agricultural racial formations, the end result being that the ownership and operation of US farms remains in primarily white hands (Minkoff-Zern et al. 2011). Even when farmers of color succeed in climbing the so-called agricultural ladder, their social positioning means that they do so with limited resources and varying level of success.

As my own research regarding the agricultural census shows, immigrant and other Latino/a farmers continue to be left out of national counts. This means they are not being recognized for their role in the food system and in particular, as farmers of color, creating new kinds of spaces and practices in the US food system. As I discuss in the next chapter, this lack of recognition is representative of a larger system of discrimination that immigrant farmers are currently facing. While they are thriving in many ways, present-day struggles, as rooted in historical inequalities, continue to create a racialized barrier to entry for many farmers.

3 Institutions, Standardization, and Markets: Hungry for Opportunity in US Agriculture

Following a USDA staff member in her white sedan with government plates, my research assistant and I drove our own unmarked rental car through a winding country highway. We passed corn and soybean fields, farmhouses, and a small downtown with a few local businesses. We drove up a gravel driveway and parked behind the USDA car. Trailing the staff member, a white female soil conservationist who had organized our visit, we walked unannounced onto a farm with a few acres of diverse vegetables, a farmhouse, a shed, and a hoop house. The hoop house had been financed through a grant from the USDA's NRCS, giving the staff member rights to visit to inspect the structure and property randomly for the first three years in order to validate that it is up to code and being used properly.

USDA staff in the Northern Neck of Virginia promote the hoop house, or "high tunnel," installation program to local vegetable farmers. These tunnel-shaped greenhouses allow farmers to start their seeds and get crops to market earlier in the season. The USDA covers the entire cost of the hoop house. In exchange, the farmer must agree to keep it in production for a minimum of three years, maintain meticulous records of their growing practices and finances, and allow USDA officials onto their property unannounced. This program is one of a variety of financial assistance opportunities for small- and medium-scale fruit and vegetable farmers through the NRCS and FSA. These agencies offer a variety of loans, grants, and crop insurance programs, which vary from year to year. Although the USDA targets historically discriminated against populations, including Latino/as, as part of its Socially Disadvantaged Groups Grant program for guaranteed, direct operating, and direct farm loans, not many immigrant farmers take advantage of these funds.

The farm we visited is owned and operated by one of a small number of Mexican immigrant farmers who directly participate in a USDA-funded program. Latino/a farmers have a low rate of inclusion in USDA programs nationally. According to the census, self-identified Hispanic or Latino/a farmers utilized USDA loans and other direct assistance programs at about one-third to one-half the rate of white farmers. In 2012, the census recorded 79,807 farm operators of Hispanic/Latino origin. One hundred and sixty-five Commodity Credit Corporation loans, 3,244 Conservation Reserve, Wetlands Reserve, Farmable Wetlands, or Conservation Reserve Enhancement program payments, and 13,276 other federal farm program payments were awarded to Latino/a operators. Respectively, that indicates a 0.2, 4, and 17 percent, respectively, inclusion rate for each program. Comparatively, the census recorded 2,034,439 white farm operators in 2012. White farm operators participated in the same loan programs at a rate of 0.6, 14, and 34 percent, respectively (USDA 2014). Those included in this count are legally in the United States, and are already engaged in some way with a government or other agricultural institution. As I discussed in the last chapter, most immigrant farmers I interviewed were unaware of the census. Therefore, I would estimate their inclusion rate in these programs is actually much lower than the census data reports.

It is not only USDA programs that immigrant farmers are underutilizing. Agricultural institutions, including state resources such as university extension services, and even nonprofit organizations, such as farmers markets and organic certification groups, which are focused on supporting alternative farmers, are not as easily accessed by immigrant farmers as they are by white farmers due to the fact that their practices are often incompatible with the standardization and bureaucracy required to be properly acknowledged as well as supervised by such organizations. I show how immigrant farmers' approach to cultivating, including their lack of record keeping, aversion to paperwork, small scale of operation, and planting of diverse crops, stands in contrast to the dominant and institutionalized alternative models of US agriculture.

This chapter addresses why immigrant farmers are so unlikely to participate in agricultural institutions and assistance programs, despite their growth as a new group of farmers. In the following chapter, I continue to draw on immigrant farmer interviews in addition to focused interviews with institutional staff, including dozens of employees of the USDA, university agricultural extension agencies, and other agricultural nongovernmental organizations, such as farmers markets and outreach groups. I contend that the standardization of practices and bureaucracy inherent in engaging with these organizations stands in stark opposition to the agrarian norms and practices of immigrant farmers, and acts to hinder their participation. The requirements of standardization help to maintain a racialized class boundary in US agriculture today and play a large role in preventing immigrant farmers from moving up the agricultural ladder.

It is not simply the size or scale of their farms that bars them from accessing resources such as those available from the USDA and university extension services, or taking advantage of opportunities such as local markets and certification, although that certainly limits what is available to them. As I discussed in the introductory chapter, the farmers in this study have limited formal education, literacy, and English-language skills, and therefore are exceptionally daunted by the paperwork necessary to apply for institutional support such as government grants, loans, and insurance. Language barriers and uneven formal educational experience aggravate their general wariness of government authority even further. Even nongovernmental institutions, such as farmers markets and organic certifiers, require paperwork, licensing, and standardization of sales.

Additionally, it is not routine for immigrant farmers to record and track their own farming progress and decisions in writing. In contrast, their farming knowledge tends to be documented and disseminated through word of mouth. Their own agricultural practices and ways of sharing knowledge also are not easily recorded in given forms. Their planting schedules and cultivation cycles tend to not fit the standardized format that paperwork often requires. It is this lack of translation, both linguistic and cultural, that functions to keep immigrant farmers away from government offices and other institutional spaces.

As has been the case for other farmers who do not replicate state-sanctioned or dominant forms of farming, these practices and forms of agrarian knowledge sharing may be interpreted as unscientific, or "illegible" to the state, and thus not deemed worthy of acknowledgment (Scott 1998), or in this case, acceptable for funding, or acceptance in formal agricultural markets and spaces. Similar arguments have been made specifically regarding Indo-Hispano practices in the US Southwest. While Hispano communities contribute to sustainable or regenerative agropastoral practices, their land-based practices have been largely shared though customary and oral traditions, which are largely unrecognizable to the state as well as environmental advocates and researchers (Peña 1999). Many small-scale diversified crop and vegetable farmers run up against such challenges when looking for government resources and support, yet for the immigrant farmers in this study, the expectation for standardized practices are compounded with the abovementioned lack of formal education, literacy, and English-language abilities. These barriers are made worse by their distrust of US government agencies and related institutions in terms of their immigration experiences.

For undocumented farmers in particular, the process of starting their own farm business may be more than merely intimidating; it may be impossible, as their status may prohibit them from officially registering their operation. To establish a farm, an aspiring farmer must go through a lengthy process of registering their land and business with the state. In order to buy land, one must also purchase a property title. There are several layers added to these basic requirements, such as liability insurance, an operator ID under which all farm inputs get recorded (also acquired through the agriculture commissioner), Occupational Safety and Health Administration registrations, and in some states, workers' compensation. Although regulations for farming, especially those regarding chemical use and labor, are important in maintaining humane and environmentally sound conditions for workers and consumers, some have been unjustly applied and interpreted to the detriment of nonwhite immigrant farmers, particularly Hmong farmers, who utilize primarily family labor and are not easily categorized given current labor regulations (Minkoff-Zern et al. 2011; Sowerwine, Getz, and Peluso 2015). Further, for some immigrants, a perceived expectation of documented immigration states, even when not actually required, such as a USDA or other institutions' office, may create fear, preventing them from entering into such a space to begin with.

If they want access to alternative farming spaces for marketing and selling their crops, immigrant farmers' struggle in providing documentation may create an added barrier. For example, if farmers want to sell their product as certified organic, they must have an organic registration from the agriculture commissioner's office as well as organic certification (through a third party). In order to sell at certified farmers markets, they must apply for various certifications and permits, depending on their product and the state they are selling in. For most of these permits, farmers must present their personal ID, tax ID, and/or social security number.

All these formal registrations require precisely the type of paperwork an undocumented person often lacks. Some use the documentation they have, such as a foreign passport or state ID card, which is available to undocumented people in some states. But for most, who do not want to use their real information due to fear of raising a red flag about their existence, especially in today's threatening political environment, they frequently rely on those with documentation to sign paperwork, take out loans, and act as legal partners for their business. Ultimately, it is not apparent as to whether legal status (or the lack thereof) strictly limits access to markets, since requirements differ by states and even specific markets' policies, and some undocumented farmers may be willing to use family members' documented status for access, while others may not. In any case, such restrictions function to increase the likelihood of immigrant farmers' exclusion from institutional settings as well as dependence on and connectedness to their family and hometown networks.

Standardization, Race, and Agricultural Institutions

The dominant industrial model promoted by the USDA, and reinforced by agricultural commodity chains, has long been problematic for small holding farmers as well as more diversified growers, regardless of race, ethnicity, or citizenship status. As Earl Butz, the secretary of agriculture under Richard Nixon, infamously told the country, farmers should "get big or get out." Butz's policies and those of the USDA leadership since have focused on supporting the large-scale production of commodity crops, corn and soy in particular, mainly through commodity price supports and crop insurance programs. These decisions are not made solely at the agency level. Agricultural policy is largely set by the US Farm Bill, which is voted on by Congress every five years. The Farm Bill sets priorities and outlines fiscal parameters for the US agricultural system as a whole. Due to large-scale lobbying and the associated influence of industrial agriculture, the Farm Bill contributes to the prioritization of large-scale industrial production, and de-prioritizes the needs of smallholders, "specialty" crop growers (mainly fruit and vegetable producers), and other diversified growers (see, among others, Ahearn, Yee, and Korb 2005; Clapp 2012; Dimitri, Effland, and Conklin 2005; DuPuis 2002).

The relationship between racial exclusion and the standardization and industrialization of farming in the United States can be traced through the exclusion of people of color from farming throughout US history. As discussed in chapter 2, African American farmers in the United States, like Latino/a and other immigrant farmers of color, have been displaced from their livelihoods many times over. According to Pete Daniel (2013), systematic discrimination by the USDA contributed to black farmers' 93 percent decline from 1940 to 1974. He argues that black farmers' cultivation techniques were seen as adversarial to the modernist vision of agriculture in the 1930s. They generally operated small, subsistence-based farms, and agricultural knowledge was passed through the generations by word of mouth.

The New Deal's Agricultural Adjustment Administration worked to make the "rural countryside legible" by compiling information and statistics on farms across the nation (ibid., 9). Large farms and grid-like orderly homesteads were idealized as the form to spread modern agricultural technologies. The USDA proceeded to map, structure, and make the rural United States visible in order to ensure a transition to agrarian efficiency. Black farming operations did not fit this model of efficiency and modernism, and therefore were not considered for subsidies and grants. Due to competition from industrial farmers with government support, thousands of black farmers were dispossessed from their land over the following decades. This preferential treatment functioned in conjunction with explicit racist conduct (ibid.).

Miriam Wells's (1996) research on the struggle of Mexican immigrants in California agriculture in the 1970s and 1980s confirms historic commonalities between African American and Latino/a immigrant farmers in terms of how their farming practices contrast with more standardized state-farming models. My own findings, described below, also reflect Wells's conclusions: Mexican and other Latino/a immigrants prefer to make their farming decisions independently, and find technical advice from government outsiders unsuitable to their own experiences and practices. Additionally, Wells (ibid., 138) observes that immigrants' lack of material resources and formal education to invest in their farm businesses leads them to be more dependent on particular "knowledge systems," which differentiate them from white farmers.

Conversely, scholars have argued that the USDA has gone through periods of democratic planning and resource distribution in some regions, as shown in the work of many agency leaders and other individuals who have worked explicitly with farmers of color, especially African American farmers. Contrasting with Daniel, Jess Gilbert (2015) specifically addresses the ways that various arms of the USDA have historically engaged people of color in land-use planning and for resource distribution. Similarly, Richard Couto (1991) has shown the ways that the FSA worked with black farmers during the New Deal era to help them transition from tenant to owner. Both these studies point to the importance of recognizing variation among USDA actors and branches. As such a large government agency, there is no one consistent way that staff or leadership interacts with the public, and certainly such successes are worth noting. Unfortunately, my research demonstrates that these historical moments in the USDA have been brief, and have not sustained a comprehensive approach to democratizing land access and ownership across racial lines in the United States.

More recent research conducted by academics as well as extension and government agencies reinforce my own findings: USDA and state/university extension programs do not provide the same quality or quantity of services to Latino/a and immigrant farmers as they do to white farmers. These other studies cover states not included in my own research, such as Missouri, Nebraska, Florida, Texas, and New Mexico, and confirm what I have found: Latino/a farmers largely do not know about services and other opportunities available through government and nonprofit agencies, and if they are aware, they misunderstand the programs and requirements. All these studies also confirmed that even when government and extension professionals are conscious of such gaps in service, they do not have the needed time or budget availability to improve their outreach or training. Further, Latino/a farmers do not tend to be as well networked with agencies and organizations compared to white farmers, and staff do not know how to locate them (Lucht 2006; Martinez and Gomez 2011; Martinez-Feria 2011; Swisher, Brennan, and Shah 2006–2007; Starkweather et al. 2011). Specific to USDA services and credit, studies have found that lacking previous credit, financial records, and business plans, being intimidated by required paperwork and a lack of support to complete such paperwork, as well as loans being geared toward larger-scale farmers were additional limitations for both immigrant and US-born Latino/a farmers (Martinez and

Gomez 2011; Martinez-Feria 2011; Swisher, Brennan, and Shah 2006–2007; Starkweather et al. 2011).

In today's USDA, despite the generally industrial agrarian focus of current funds, there are some opportunities for small-scale farmers as well as those who have been deemed sustainable or socially disadvantaged by the agency. The Sustainable Agriculture Research and Education program provides USDA-sponsored grants and outreach in each state. Moreover, the USDA conducts research and development related to regional food initiatives, such as farmers markets, which are the primary markets for the immigrant farmers included in this study. The USDA also manages the Cooperative State Research, Education, and Extension Service, which supports research and outreach through regional offices as well as the Land-Grant University System. The mission of the extension services is to bring research-based information conducted in university settings to the public, with a large focus on agrarian communities. Unfortunately, like the USDA more broadly, the land-grant system along with related research and extension have been heavily critiqued for their connection to and bias toward industrial and corporate agriculture (Kloppenburg 2005; Welsh and Glenna 2006). The USDA also sponsors the Beginning Farmer and Rancher Development Program, which includes funds and loan programs potentially available to new immigrant farmers. Yet as Adam Calo (2018) argues, this program takes a knowledge-deficient approach, attempting to teach farmers technical and entrepreneurial skills, rather than addressing the structural, race and ethnicity, and language barriers that immigrant farmers encounter. And I would further contend, as long as USDA outreach has no specific focus on immigrant and other Latino/a farmers, these farmers will not know how to go about accessing such resources, even when they are applicable.

Over the course of conducting this research, I have encountered USDA and extension staff who are actively engaged with farming communities of color, and some who specifically outreach to Mexican-born and other Latino/a immigrant farmers. These staff members' level of commitment to immigrant farmers varies based on the region and prevalence of immigrant farmers as well as resources they had available to extend. Unfortunately, these practices were not the norm, and the staff who actively pursued opportunities to work with Latino/a immigrant or other minority farmers expressed that there was a lack of structural support from their agencies in that pursuit. Although there are programs targeted to sustainable or diverse growers, this information cannot reach farmers if they are not on the radar of the state in the first place. As discussed above, this kind of structural discrimination in the USDA is by no means new. By systematically targeting only white or what USDA staff call "traditional" farmers, and not addressing racialized disparities within the agency's current methods of resource distribution, the historical discrimination so well documented by Daniel (2013) and others will only continue.

Further, differential historic migration patterns oftentimes lead to unequal access to federal resources at the state and regional level for immigrant farmers. When I was able to interview regionally based USDA outreach staff, they were often aware of the immigrant farmer presence in the area as well as their absence of participation in state-funded programs. Yet engagement with and outreach to immigrant farming communities by the USDA varies greatly by region, and is usually determined by the number of bilingual staff in the regional offices. Since there is no national mandate and limited focus on hiring multilingual staff, outreach and immigrant participation depends on who applies for positions more broadly. Of course, in regions with more established Latino/a populations, there is a higher chance that there will be a Spanish-speaking staff member. But in newer immigrant communities, there is little likelihood that there will be someone who can communicate with immigrant farmers. Although all farmers should hypothetically have access to similar USDA resources and programs, given regional growing patterns, having a bilingual staff member to make those resources available and understandable is dependent on social integration between immigrants and their new communities.

In Washington State, for example, I met with two Spanish-speaking FSA officers, both of whom do significant outreach with immigrant farmers. This was the only place where I found and interviewed USDA staff who were able to communicate with monolingual Spanish-speaking immigrant farmers during my research.[1] Also in Washington State, I met with several extension agents through the Washington State University Center for Sustaining Agriculture and Natural Resources who were actively conducting research with and securing resources for Latino/a farmers specifically. In contrast, in the Northern Neck of Virginia and Hudson Valley of New York, I found no Spanish-speaking staff in the FSA or NRCS offices, despite the large presence of Mexican immigrants farming in the region. When

I conducted interviews in Virginia, the local university extension agent spoke minimal Spanish and helped immigrant farmers access educational materials, but said she was unable to entice them to apply for USDA funds or programs.[2]

A regionally based USDA staff member told me that there must be 10 percent participation in USDA programs in the region for bilingual forms to be made available. It is unlikely, however, that there will ever be more than 10 percent participation if the paperwork is not made available in Spanish in the first place. This catch-22 represents a structural problem within the USDA, aggravating the already-tenuous history of USDA discrimination. Although Spanish-speaking immigrants comprise the majority of the workforce on US farms, there is little support from the government in helping them transition to better-paying or more reputable positions in agriculture. The structural conditions that maintain racialized immigrants in low-income agrarian positions function to maintain white control over our food system at large.

Finally, the nongovernmental organizations I studied, such as farmers markets—although unlike agricultural governmental institutions, may prioritize alternative forms of farming—still struggle to include immigrant farmers and other farmers of color. Despite immigrants' mode of farming fitting within the framework of alternative production, which generally garners a higher selling price, the immigrant farmers are not getting the same increased share of the dollar from the organic and local farming movement compared to white farmers. Based on my interviews and observations at farmers markets in all these regions, immigrant farmers are generally less likely to be certified organic (and therefore unable to charge the price premiums associated with organic certification). Many immigrant farmers struggle to enter markets in higher-paying neighborhoods, which they find to be largely inaccessible to them.[3] Although I did meet many farmers market managers who were actively supporting the immigrant farming community, they discussed the challenges with me in helping farmers meet consumer expectations and cultural norms, rather than the other way around.

Most of the farmers I spoke with were selling primarily at farmers markets. A handful had started community-supported agriculture programs, and one was considering a u-pick, although those farmers tended to have better English and literacy skills and/or adult children to help them. Since their farms are small scale, and they are cultivating a diversity of crops, they are limited to marketplaces where there is an emphasis on product variety. This restricts them to direct sales outlets such as farmers markets, or selling specialty crops in small batches to restaurants and small grocery stores. Additionally, selling directly to customers allows them to maintain a certain level of control over production without being beholden to wholesalers or other large buyers. This is a familiar way for them to grow and sell—most similar to their family practices selling in open-air markets in Mexico.

Several researchers have found that farmers markets in particular can be exclusionary to people of color, as their participants consist of well-connected communities of white farmers and consumers (Alkon 2008, 2012; Alkon and McCullen 2011; Slocum 2008). Actors who commonly participate in US farmers markets, including vendors, managers, and customers, frequently reflect a "pervasive whiteness," which permeates farmers market environments. Farmers market culture prioritizes liberal, affluent values such as making social change via purchasing power and self-improvement through healthy diets (Alkon and McCullen 2011). This research illuminates the challenges that immigrant farmers face, yet it focuses on consumer perspectives, not farmers. In this chapter, I build on such studies by providing an analysis of the experience of farmers of color. In doing so, I create a more complete picture of farmers market and broader food system inequity.

Agricultural institutions, from the USDA to farmers markets, maintain racial and ethnic disparities on a structural level. In what follows, I shed light on the ways that such institutions' processes are promoted as universally accessible or free from racial bias, despite such divides. I explore how government and nonprofit expectations of standardization largely function as gatekeepers to agricultural development and growth, notwithstanding individual and structural efforts to create inclusivity.

Lawsuits, Discrimination, and Improving Outreach

In response to a number of civil rights lawsuits against the USDA on behalf of African American, Hispanic, Native American, and female farmers over the past fifteen years, the US secretary of agriculture under President Obama, Thomas Vilsack (2009), proclaimed a "new era of civil rights" for the agency. These lawsuits targeted the USDA, documenting the ways that farmers of color have been structurally discriminated against by the agency. In 1999, two class action lawsuits, *Pigford v. Glickman* and *Brewington v. Glickman*, were settled by African American farmers alleging racial discrimination by the USDA between 1981 and 1996 while applying for farm loans and assistance. The *Keepseagle v. Vilsack* case was then settled for Native American farmers who claimed discrimination by the agency between 1981 and 1999. In 2000, yet another class action suit was filed against the USDA—this time on behalf of Hispanic farmers and ranchers who were discriminated against from 1981 to 2000, also while applying for USDA loans. The USDA admitted to discrimination, and this case was settled via a claims process in which farmers were eligible to receive from $50,000 to $250,000 (Hispanic and Women Farmers and Ranchers Claims and Resolution Process 2012; Martinez and Gomez 2011).

National outreach for the claims process was conducted during summer 2013 via television and radio ads. Those who claimed eligibility were meant to fill out forms online. Although lawyers were not technically needed to file a claim, the process was complicated, requiring a variety of forms and documentation. The USDA employees I spoke with said they recommended legal assistance in order to properly submit a claim. With assistance from the Farmers Legal Action Group and National Agricultural Law Center, the USDA trained lawyers to help with the claims, but individuals still had to compensate the attorneys out of pocket—an unreasonable cost for most small-scale Latino/a farmers. According to a USDA Inspector General Audit Report, the USDA received approximately 54,000 claims, yet 32,000 were considered incomplete or late. Ultimately only 3,176, less than 6 percent of all claims, were approved (Harden 2016). One media source reported that a one-line explanation was provided to farmers whose claims were not accepted: "You failed to provide sufficient documentation, or the documentation that you provided was not sufficient to meet the requirements under the framework" (Zippert 2015). As I discuss below, this statement reflects many immigrant farmers' general lack of standardization and documentation practices, which are necessary in order to be deemed legible in the eyes of the USDA.

Although some Latino/a farmers will be reimbursed through the claims process for profits lost, most were not made aware of the claims process or their right to file as part of the suit. According to agents at regional FSA offices in Washington State, they were given a script response to anyone inquiring about the process locally, and the outreach to farmers was

NOTICE TO HISPANIC AND/OR WOMEN FARMERS OR RANCHERS

COMPENSATION FOR CLAIMS OF DISCRIMINATION

If you believe that the United States Department of Agriculture (USDA) improperly denied farm loan benefits to you between 1981 and 2000 because you are Hispanic, or because you are female, you may be eligible to apply for compensation. This means you may be eligible if:

1. you sought a farm loan or farm-loan servicing during that period; and

2. the loan was denied, provided late, approved for a lesser amount than requested, or approved with restrictive conditions, or USDA failed to provide an appropriate loan service; and

3. you believe these actions were based on your being Hispanic, or your being female.

If you want to register your name to receive a claims packet, you can call the Farmer and Rancher Call Center at 1-888-508-4429 or access the following website: www.farmerclaims.gov

In 2011, a claims administrator will begin mailing claims packages to those who have requested one through the Call Center or website. The claims package will have detailed information about the eligibility and claims process.

For guidance, you may contact a lawyer or other legal services provider in your community.

If you are currently represented by counsel regarding allegations of discrimination or in a lawsuit claiming discrimination, you should contact your counsel regarding this claims process.

USDA Cannot Provide Legal Advice to You.

USDA is an equal opportunity provider and employer.

USDA — United States Department of Agriculture

Figure 3.1

Notice posted in USDA local offices to outreach to farmers regarding the Hispanic and women farmers and ranchers discrimination claims process.

contracted out to a private firm.⁴ When I asked their counterparts in Virginia and New York about outreach, they told me that they had flyers in the office, but no one had applied. These are the same offices where they told me Latino/a farmers rarely visit. Of the farmers I interviewed, most stated they had never applied for USDA funds or entered its offices, thereby making the claims process irrelevant in rectifying the type of structural discrimination they may have faced.

Those who experienced discrimination after 2000 were not able to submit a claim. Even at the federal level, where the secretary of agriculture at the time of the claims process maintained they were ushering in a "new era" at the USDA, a former federal staff member at the USDA's Socially Disadvantaged Farmer and Rancher Program expressed to me that most of the changes to address discrimination are equivalent to offering "coffee and donuts" rather than dealing with the roots of the problem. In her opinion, the USDA's claims of making institutional change to combat historic discrimination are merely rhetoric put in place to improve the agency's image. The program does not provide technical assistance that farmers really need:

> "Here, have a cookie and some coffee; honest, we'll give you a loan." But then they leave. And actually, "No honest, we won't give you a loan," because nobody actually stopped eating the donut and the coffee, and figured out how to get financed, because that would be hard work. ... "Here's information about the USDA. Hey, by the way, the USDA doesn't discriminate anymore. And we really hope that when you come to our office, you'll meet someone who looks like you and treats you with respect, and if they don't, here's your civil rights." But not, "So let's sit down with your tax return now."

In her opinion, although there is a genuine intention of creating more racially just programs from the top levels of the administration (or there was, during her time there under the Vilsack administration), in effect, the USDA's claims of making institutional change to combat historic discrimination are merely oratory performance. She argues that to improve opportunities for disadvantaged farmers, they need technical assistance with their finances. For immigrants who have experience working in the fields, but do not have a background in business or a family member to teach them, technical skills, such as bookkeeping and business planning, tend to be the primary constraints to maintaining a functioning business.

Although the claims process is evidence of an effort to improve race relations at the federal level, discrimination often occurs in local offices.

Local-level discrimination is rarely addressed in the national USDA headquarters. Of the immigrant farmers I interviewed who grow using alternative methods, only a handful have successfully used USDA programs. Of the diverse crop producers, two had grants for hoop houses from the NRCS, and one had crop insurance, secured through his local USDA's Risk Management Agency (RMA) office.[5] Those with hoop house grants have used them to extend their growing season in Virginia, although this has been a struggle due to the lengthy application paperwork and requirement for growing practices to be continually tracked.

Martin, a farmer in Virginia, applied for a hoop house and had been accepted into the program, but at the time of our last interview, had yet to receive the funds. He is originally from Guadalajara, Mexico, where his family still owns agricultural land. He came to the United States when he was twenty-one years old. Once he arrived in the United States, he spent twenty-seven years working in agriculture before saving the money to start his own farm. When we met, he had been operating his own farm for three years. He emphasized the importance of his family's help and labor in keeping the farm profitable.

Martin's daughter, Claudia, discussed their experience trying to get access to hoop house funding. Claudia was educated in the United States, and speaks and writes in perfect English—a valuable skill for her family in terms of accessing potential resources. After not getting funding on her first try, she started questioning why her family's farm didn't receive aid when other farmers around her did:

> I went to the local NRCS office to ask about funds for building a hoop house. They told me in the office that they did not currently have funds, so I couldn't apply. … [Later, I told] this to a [white] customer at the market who had worked for the USDA. She told me they should still take my application. The customer contacted the office for me, and they then told me to come in and to get an application. In the meantime, I noticed that other [white] neighbors were receiving the funding, while I was turned away. I applied, and we eventually [were approved for] the funding, although we are still waiting for it to go through.

When I asked if he thought there was discrimination against immigrant or Latino/a farmers, Diego, a farmer in California, explained that he believes that USDA officials don't think immigrants will follow through with their plans.

Well honestly, yes. They've always looked at us with that label, "He is a foreigner, his accent ..." They always push you aside, especially when you go to organizations like [the] USDA ... because they want a plan, yes? Let's just say that the government sends money for agriculture for some counties. And then you arrive, and since you are new and there are other farmers who know how the system works, they know quickly what they have to do.

Diego expresses the belief that because there are other farmers with more established relationships with the USDA, the staff will choose to work with them over a newcomer, who they are unsure about. The notion of a "plan" is one that came up in conversations with farmers and organizational staff alike throughout my research. Immigrant farmers are less likely to record and track their progress, and government agencies and nonprofits need such records or plans in order to work with farmers, as evidence of their past and projected success.[6] I met Alejandro at a farmers market in a northern suburb of Seattle. A heavyset, middle-aged man, he has been farming in Washington State for over a decade and now mentors many younger immigrant farmers. Alejandro came to the United States in 1978 from Colima, Mexico, where he learned how to farm from his family and still owns agricultural land. Before owning and operating his own farm in the United States, he worked in grape and orange harvests up and down the West Coast. Alejandro recounted changes he has observed over the past several decades for immigrant farmers, not just in Washington State, but in places like California.

Although he is documented and owns his land, Alejandro feels that because many immigrants are undocumented, USDA staff are biased against any immigrant or Latino/a when they walk into an agency office. "There are many Latinos without papers," says Alejandro, "and there can be discrimination because of that." In his view, because some immigrants are unable to produce the necessary documents to work with the agency, staff will assume any immigrant is a waste of their time, without knowing their immigration status.

The same former federal USDA staff member reaffirmed this kind of racial discrimination at local offices: "Now some of what happens today, when there is actually overt racism, it's still not as overt. It's more like, 'Oh, your forms aren't complete.' And they'll hold [nonwhite] persons' forms to higher scrutiny than they would a white person's forms."

Of course, not all immigrants feel that they are discriminated against. Antonia, a farmer in Virginia, grew up in Tamaulipas, Mexico, where she learned to farm with her family. Living in a border state, Antonia migrated back and forth to the United States with her family from an early age. When she was eighteen years old, she and her family decided to stay and work in agriculture full time. In the early 1990s, Antonia and her husband started their own business, renting farmland. At the time of our interview, they were in the process of getting a loan through the FSA so they could finally purchase the land they farm on. Antonia, who speaks English well, noted that she received a lot of help when she looked into getting a loan from the USDA: "When I filled out the application for the FSA, she helped me a lot, the lady in Fredericksburg. ... She helped me go through all the paperwork—what I needed to fax her or bring her by. It was easy. Because she helped me a lot. And she told us that there were a lot of programs for Hispanic females. She looked into what categories I qualified for."

Antonia added that her challenge in getting resources was less about the individuals working in the offices and more about structural limitations, such as literacy, which I discuss more in the section below.

Other farmers described experiences that they felt were discriminatory in looking for traditional bank loans. Ricardo, an established farmer in Virginia, learned to farm during his childhood in Michoacán, Mexico, where he and his family still own land. When Ricardo came to the United States, he worked as a laborer on multiple farms up and down the East Coast before settling in the Northern Neck region of Virginia. At the time of our interview, he had owned his farm business for almost seven years. Ricardo discussed his challenges in accessing a bank loan to expand his farm:

> I've seen a lot of [white] people who go and ask for help, and they [the bank] give it to them, but they don't give it to us. This year, I put in a lot of applications to buy land, and they will put it under the desk and never look at it. Sometimes I would go and ask about it, and they'll tell me that they didn't look at it. I told them they better give it back to me. I went to other banks with my application. ... They never even saw it. I already paid for my land, I just wanted to add more, but they didn't even look at it. I did feel discriminated against; they didn't even look at it.

He expressed that because of the fact that he is clearly a Latino immigrant, the loan officers assumed he would not be applicable for a loan and did not consider his application, despite the fact that he is financially eligible.

Norma, an established farmer in California, has owned her farming operation for over twenty years. After immigrating to California from the Mexican state of Guerrero in 1986, she spent almost a decade picking produce in the Salinas Valley. In 1994, she was one of the first graduates of ALBA's new farmer training program. She is now somewhat of an icon in the organic farming world in California, widely known as the first immigrant Latina farmworker to start her own certified organic farm in the state. She also founded a nonprofit to help other immigrant farmers acquire organic certification and apply for support programs. Despite these accomplishments, when I interviewed her, she still had not succeeded in getting USDA assistance herself. She explained her experience visiting her local offices, telling me, "If you go to an agency and you are a Latina person, and you are a woman, and you don't speak the language, and you don't have money, and you are going to an agency of the federal government and you want to find someone to speak your language, how do you say this? ... The government doesn't want to help you. It doesn't want to have a person who speaks your language."

As she remarks, immigrants are made to feel belittled—that their place is working in the fields, not in the government offices or management positions on a farm. David is also a well-established certified organic farmer in California, having graduated from the ALBA program at the same time as Norma. He brought up the discrimination that he experienced at the USDA offices before I even inquired. David stated that when he went to his local FSA office, they seemed biased toward white farmers who have owned their businesses longer, and have more developed business and planting plans as well as proof of their sales. He got the feeling they wanted him to leave and were uninterested in investing time in him.

In regions with no bilingual staff, USDA employees informed me that few immigrant farmers enter their offices, although the "local," "traditional," or white farmers usually come and ask for what they need. At the NRCS in Virginia, I was told,

> They don't know about the cover crop program, they don't know about the high tunnel program if it doesn't go to their mailbox. Because I don't see them at all, unless I go to their farm. They don't come in here unless they hear about the program from their neighbor, or brother, or sister, or something. They just don't walk in here like most of my clients do. They're [white farmers] in here all the time. They're calling all the time, "Can you help me get funded?" And they [immigrant farmers] never do that.

In New York State, the FSA agent was aware of the needs of the immigrant farming community. He lamented the FSA's limitations as an office to outreach to immigrant farmers, and faulted his agency's slim budget for contacting new and minority farmers,

> We obviously have, like most federal governments, limited budgets for doing certain things such as outreach, so the primary tools that we have available to us are email listservs, which you have to be signed up to get, and then newsletters, which are mailed out to and targeted toward producers whom we currently know about. So if you've never come into our office, if you've never signed up for any of our listings, chances are you've not heard of us or the services we offer. So that is the biggest limitation that we have in our outreach efforts. ... Ideally, we'd love to have a budget that allowed us to go out to farmers markets in the area on every Sunday or Saturday, but you know, we just don't have resources for that.

It is clear from offices that work closely with immigrant farmers that their outreach specifically to the Spanish-speaking immigrant community has had to be intentional and concerted. Ostrom, introduced in the preceding chapter, is the director of the Small Farm Program for Washington State University. In her work at the center, she has committed herself to doing outreach to Latino/a farmers specifically:

> I've gotten grants over the years to try to make that, we call it a "welcoming space," a bilingual space. We have to reeducate them [extension staff] and reeducate them because they are like, "Why don't any of them come?" Well, we have to go and do all this outreach, we have to explain, they need to know somebody there. So [the incubator] Viva Farms has been great; they always have that person there, they have Kate or Robert who the farmers are friends with. ... You have to do the outreach, you have to do the extra calling, you have to have your flyers, you have to call people.

She reaffirms the need for outreach, and refers to the collaborative relationship between regional extension staff and the local farm incubator program, Viva Farms. As she makes clear, immigrant farmers, and others who are not usually welcome in government and/or mainstream agricultural spaces as farmers, will not seek out the resources that are available to them. Those who manage the resources need to actively find them.

Ostrom has developed a program for small farmers in Washington State that specifically focuses on Spanish-speaking farmers. Although she is committed to fund-raising and outreach to help them develop their business and get extension support, she sees many challenges that differ from those of white beginning farmers in terms of providing that support:

Just getting to educational programs when you have problems with transportation and childcare, working full time with someone else, when you don't control your schedule. It's hard for them to say, "Oh, I have a class on Tuesday and I can't make it to work." So those kinds of challenges. They don't know how to write the applications, they don't know how to make business plans. We spend a lot of time in developing record keeping, application forms, big challenges.

Ultimately, she argues, to successfully outreach to the immigrant community, extension and other service providers need consistent bilingual staff, and institutional support where they are able to build relationships. Ostrom explains that it is more than just a temporary linguistic translation; rather, it's about building a strong link between the agency and the community of farmers that they wish to reach. "I thought that they really need the bilingual staff, but it was about the relationship in the community," observes Ostrom. "If you just hire people in this grant and that grant, they don't know people."

Yet the way extension is structured, expectations for agents are based on the number of farmers they meet with and revenue those farmers bring in, which creates an additional challenge to extending needed support to immigrants, since it takes time to build trust and the networks in their communities. As Ostrom explains, "We have to convince our administrators that it is all right to spend more time with fewer farmers. With the incubator program—they will look at those numbers and then will be like, 'Well that's only seven farmers, and they're not even their own farms yet, and you've already put all this time in and money.' So the metrics they're using, they don't work well for small farms because they're measuring how many acres of production, they're measuring how many farmers."

Comments from the bilingual USDA staff members in Washington State reflected Ostrom's arguments regarding the importance of relationship building to reach immigrant farmers. Both emphasized that the work they do with the immigrant community is dependent on their own social networks as well as the trust they have been able to build with the farmworker community over time. José Limon, the son of a farmworker turned farmer who now works as a senior farm loan officer at the FSA office in Wenatchee, Washington, told me that "it takes the relationships. ... I think that's because if they know you, if they know your family, or it is in the community, they are more likely to trust if they know somebody. ... I'm not just going to come in; they're probably going to ask some questions before."

Crispin Garza is an FSA loan specialist in Yakima County. As far as he is aware, he and José are the only Spanish-speaking USDA employees in Washington State. He told me that before he came to work at the USDA twenty-seven years ago, there were no Latino/as employed in the office, and there was a definite language barrier. No Mexicans came to the office, he said. "They were afraid to talk to the Anglos." He reiterated the importance of word of mouth and community relationships in developing these professional relationships and opportunities for farmers. From his perspective, to build trust in the nonwhite immigrant community, even among those who are documented, there must be continued institutional support, as many are skeptical of the US government and white people in general.

Although both Crispin and José were born in the United States, they are children of migrant farmworkers and also have experience working in the fields themselves during their youth. Both of them provide translation to immigrant farmers daily, yet this service is not part of their job description, and as Crispin explained, "I provide free translation services to the agency." He also expressed disappointment at the lack of commitment from the agency to consistently hire bilingual staff on a state or national level.

These assessments were echoed by Gabrielle Rovegno, who has worked with the immigrant farming community in Virginia for several years. Rovegno originally connected with the Latino/a farming community as an AmeriCorps VISTA volunteer. Her position took her to the Washington, DC, area to work in the Crossroads Community Food Network as its microenterprise and community kitchen coordinator. The organization manages a farmers market in the Langley Heights neighborhood of Maryland, right next to the DC border, and is expressly focused on helping ensure food security for the low-income Latino/a immigrant community that lives there. Along with managing the market and creating programs to increase food affordability, Crossroads also works closely with the vendors to support their businesses, including many immigrant farmers from the Northern Neck of Virginia. It was at this market that I met several of the farmers I interviewed and visited in Virginia. In this position, Rovegno started outreach to immigrant farmers through farm visits and training programs, working with many of the same farmers interviewed for this book. She currently works at another DC-area nonprofit called EcoCity Farms as a farm training coordinator, continuing her role doing outreach in the region, where she has also become a business partner with one of the farms included in this study.

As an outreach coordinator, she noted the farmers' lack of record keeping and promotional materials as well as their limited access to USDA and extension resources. She organized workshops to pinpoint their needs and troubleshoot solutions. When I spoke with her, one of the largest problems Rovegno identified was the need for one-on-one mentoring along with the development of personal relationships between extension and farmers. Through her position, she created a visual English/Spanish insect guide for farmers (see Rovegno 2016), seeing it as "the first step in trying to get more Hispanic/Latino farmers engaged/assured that there are culturally appropriate resources for them, and then ensuring GAP [Good Agricultural Practices certification], pesticide training, etc., is offered in Spanish." There are plans for the guide to be used by regional extension agents and sustainable agriculture groups. Additionally, Crossroads is organizing multiple all-Spanish instructional field days on integrated pest management practices across the region—the first of their kind in the area.

Another organization creating important and useful materials for Spanish-speaking farmers is the National Center for Appropriate Technology through its ATTRA Sustainable Agriculture Program. The ATTRA program creates Spanish-language resources, such as fact sheets on organic production, soil management, and crop rotation. The center also has bilingual Spanish-speaking staff and a Spanish-language hotline.[7] It is largely funded through the USDA's Rural Business Cooperative Service, providing a good example of state resources being used for creating a more inclusive agricultural system on a national scale.

To move forward from a sordid history of race relations in US agricultural institutions, more genuine efforts at outreach must become the norm. Of course, in the current political moment, increased funding as well as interest in immigrants and people of color in agriculture cannot be expected from government institutions at the federal level. Yet the path toward inclusion is a long one, and these lessons will be learned and progress will be made as long as immigrant farmers continue to make their presence known. As I argue in the concluding chapters, by creating a more inclusive alternative food and farming movement more broadly, we can apply pressure to such institutions to change over time.

Paperwork and Standardization

As mentioned previously, most immigrant farmers have had little formal education, and their literary and English-language skills vary. Many have completed elementary school, and some have completed high school—all in Spanish. While all farmers interviewed speak some English, many only speak enough to get by at a farmers market, and not much more. Their limited abilities in reading and writing, especially in English, add to their struggles in navigating the bureaucracy of the US agriculture system.

When farmers were asked what they think the greatest challenge is for immigrant farmers accessing government or other programs, including organic certification, most mentioned the paperwork. As far as working with the USDA, this discomfort stems from a general distrust of the US government, coupled with the fact that most immigrant farmers have limited English skills as well as reading and writing abilities even in their native language. As can be expected from any government institution, the USDA requires extensive paperwork before, during, and after taking advantage of its loans, grants, or insurance options. Although white farmers may also be resistant to paperwork and general bureaucracy, the fact that most farmers we interviewed did not have an education past middle school, means they are lacking the literacy skills necessary to fill out the required paperwork in any language. For many, this means they may never enter the door of an organization to inquire about opportunities due to feelings of intimidation. For others, lacking English language and literacy proficiency may be the ultimate reason they stall in the process, and thus fail to obtain the grant, loan, or insurance package.

Although some USDA forms are available online in Spanish, finding them is difficult and availability is inconsistent. Further, online availability has become even sparser during the past several years, since the advent of the Trump administration. While the NRCS national site was reasonably user friendly for Spanish speakers when I last checked, with a page specifically dedicated to the forms in Spanish, including Spanish instructions to access the forms, other agency forms and information are harder to come by for non-English speakers, and some have become less available since 2016.[8] On the FSA website, nothing is currently available in Spanish, unless you look in its "Archived Fact Sheets," where some information dating from 2014 to

2016 could be found. Even before these documents became archived, one had to go through an exhaustive search to find the translated information. To find them, the user had to go to the FSA main site, and find the link to FSA "Fact Sheets" under the "Newsroom" link, which is listened under the "FSA Home" site. The whole search had to be done in English. One then had to choose from a drop-down menu in English to get the translated links. Even then, only a small fraction of all available English documents were available translated. Currently, no updated forms are available in Spanish on the federal FSA site.[9]

Without Spanish-speaking outreach abilities, most farmers never hear about the programs available. When asked about the USDA, the farmers interviewed were unaware of opportunities accessible to them. FSA loans are designed for farmers who struggle with traditional bank loans and are meant to be a farmers' first line of credit. Although the farmers interviewed frequently told me they were unable to get access to credit from regular banks, they were unaware that USDA loan programs existed for these reasons specifically. Irma, a farmer in Virginia, relayed this lack of awareness: "The truth is that I don't know what they [the USDA] have. … We were told that in Warsaw [Virginia], in the department of environment, where the applications are, that one can fill something out so that they can give you a big greenhouse. I only learned about it this year, however. I just didn't know."

Even those who speak nearly perfect English still find the forms intimidating. One immigrant farmer, who has obtained US citizenship, told me, "I tried in the past to get a small operating loan. And I didn't feel confident enough to fill out the application by myself because there were a lot of questions I didn't know." Since attempting to apply for her first USDA loan, as described above, she has since applied for another loan, which she successfully secured with the assistance of the local FSA staff. Yet the level of confidence needed to walk into a government office where a huge stack of paperwork awaits is unrealistic for most, especially when understood in the context of the tense relationship between most rural Latino/a immigrants and the state given their histories of immigration. Although many of the farmer participants in this study are documented, some got their legal paperwork after crossing the border illegally in the early 1980s. They are all part of larger immigrant families and communities, which include both documented and undocumented individuals. If even one family member or housemate is undocumented, this may create a barrier for a farmer in engaging with government agencies for fear of putting that person on the increasingly aggressive deportation radar.

In the rare cases where immigrant farmers do succeed in getting USDA assistance, it is not necessarily an experience they would recommend to others in their same position given the barriers, time, and human resources they must expend to complete the process. José came to the United States twenty-eight years ago when he was fourteen. He immediately started working in agriculture. Even though he learned to farm in Mexico, José attributes much of his farming experience to his early years picking oranges in Florida and strawberries in New York. José has sixty acres in production and was the only farmer I interviewed who had crop insurance, which he secured through his local USDA's RMA office in Virginia. It took him three trips to the offices to get the proper paperwork filled out. He does not read nor write well in English, and found the process intimidating and frustrating. It was also time consuming, beyond what he felt he could afford. As the owner-operator of a family-run business, his physical presence was needed on his farm.

Brett Melone is the director of lending at California FarmLink, an organization that helps beginning farmers access land and financial resources. Approximately 70 percent of FarmLink's borrowers are Latino/a. In reference to RMA loans, he told me,

> While the RMA subsidizes the federal crop insurance program, crop insurance actually must be purchased through a private insurance agent, which creates an additional barrier for immigrant farmers. I have been told by RMA staff that they cannot provide names of appropriate agents [either those who write policies for Whole Farm Revenue Protection, a particular type of crop insurance that is designed for diversified operations, or those who speak Spanish]. You are basically on your own to ask other farmers or use the ineffective search tool on the RMA website to find an agent who meets your needs.

The fact that paperwork and the related language barrier are the greatest impediments to aid for immigrant farmers is well understood by USDA staff in these counties. A USDA employee in Virginia explains,

> Most of our [immigrant] producers—[we] used to have some come in the office. They don't come in anymore. I think it's English. Because we had one who couldn't speak English, and he would always bring his son in here. And then the forms. We have some forms that are in Spanish, but most of our forms aren't. I

think it's ... where they're used to dealing with more cash than a lot of paperwork. I think they find the paperwork a little overwhelming.

In addition to noting that the written forms themselves are a technical challenge, she highlights that immigrant farmers are not used to operating in bureaucratic environments. They are not accustomed to excessive paperwork from their experience as farmers in Mexico or farmworkers in the United States. This requirement can be the first barrier to entry for immigrant farmers. On seeing such a requirement, and the lack of available cultural and linguistic translation, they feel the offices are not a welcoming place for them and cease attempting to work with the agency, further limiting their access to available and appropriate resources for agrarian class advancement.

Even after the initial application for participation in a program is filed, there can be a large amount of follow-up paperwork over a long period of time. For example, to participate in the hoop house program, one farmer told us, "What you have to do is keep a log of how much you spent, what you're getting out of it, and your profit out of it. So that's something that we had to do." Another farmer who participated in the program said, "They were very strict and limited to certain stuff [that we could plant]. ... It's very complicated paperwork." They were both grateful for the program support but expressed that the paperwork was an extra burden on top of their already-busy schedules. Those who did use USDA programs also noted that their children, who are often born and educated in the United States, were typically responsible for filing this paperwork. The farmers' children were most comfortable with the language and the formalities of crop documentation, which their parents struggle to navigate. For those farmers without grown or teenage children to help with the paperwork, participation in such programs was an even greater barrier.

Robert, an FSA employee in the Hudson Valley who was introduced in chapter 2, concurred with what immigrant producers told me: "That is a challenge. There are lots of producers out there that have poor records of production, plantings, and things like that. We can work with them and try to work through those problems, but they need to, at the end of the day, come up with something that they can sort of justify."

As James C. Scott (1998) describes, the requirements of the state frequently function to reduce diverse ways of knowing and interacting with space as well as the environment. Such analysis rings true here, as immigrant farmers' ways of interpreting and tracking their own agricultural knowledge do not fit into the neat categories created by the agency, and therefore have limited legitimacy from a state perspective.

As Robert explains further, in order to get a loan or insurance, farmers need to hand over specific records of their farming practices. "The 'NAP' program, which is that crop insurance program, requires you to give us records each year of your acreage that you plant as well as your production that you get from that. So you need to come into the office, say exactly this is what I have planted, how many acres and where, and then you have to give us production to support that also."

While such records might be a reasonable request from the perspective of someone deciding who to give a loan or insurance package to, it may be the final obstacle that keeps immigrant farmers from getting such kinds of support. As their practices are not deemed legitimate by the state due to their inability to fit into and record their farming in the specific ways required, they are further limited in their access to resources, and more distance is thus created between them and the very agency meant to help them get their business established. Farmers themselves explain this disconnect below.

Rodolfo, an orchardist in Washington State, is originally from Guerrero. His father participated in the Bracero Program, staying in the United States after his position ended. Rodolfo started working in fruit-packing warehouses during his youth and continued to work in the fields for other farmers as an adult. Twelve years before we met, he had started his own farming operation. Rodolfo explains that paperwork is not intuitive to those who have been doing field work for most of their lives. While they are experienced in the technicalities of farming, filling out forms is a different and more challenging task. "It is a very drastic change if you are used to doing the [farm] work. It's easier to do the [farm] work than to be in charge of paperwork." Similarly, Ricardo, in Virginia, says that he just can't find the time to learn the process and ensure the paperwork has been filled out correctly. He is needed on the farm, and that is where he would rather be, although he knows getting institutional support would help his business. "We've been trying to go and get some stuff, because I know they'll help us. But it's been ... too much paperwork, too much involvement," he tells me. "You know, all these meetings and stuff to go through it."

Rovegno, the VISTA employee doing outreach in Virginia, discusses how she helped translate forms for immigrant growers. First, she notes, as a translator, it was difficult to find the appropriate words in Spanish:

> The National Agricultural Library's glossary uses words that are used at the highest levels of academia both in English and Spanish. UC Davis's glossary lacks many words of insects and weeds present in the Mid-Atlantic, and often has the wrong picture next to the insect name, failing to give me confidence in those translations. The most comprehensive glossary to be found was made by the US Forest Service in 1988. Many of the words reflect Mexican origin, though many farmers were not accustomed to using the words listed. This led me to compile a list of all the technical words I needed and seek input for the translation in Spanish from over ten contributors from five Spanish-speaking countries. (Rovegno 2016, 7)

Further, she found that it was not just language translation that was needed but cultural translation as well. In order for immigrant farmers to accept and process information regarding regulations and farm management practices, a peer-to-peer approach worked better than a standard classroom setting. As Rovegno (ibid., 9) described it, "To keep the farmers engaged and seen as the experts, almost the entirety of the pictures used in the presentations were taken on one of the Crossroads farmers' farms. For every picture, the farmer would have the opportunity to explain to the rest of the class what practice was being highlighted. This promoted engagement in the presentation and increased the farmer's self-esteem."

With little to no formal educational experience, but lifelong experience as experts in the fields, she found that they responded to a flipped classroom approach. In order for outreach to be successful, she had to first acknowledge the linguistic barriers, as well as the different experiences in communication and learning styles, based on years of experiential versus classroom-based learning. It was only after making these changes that she could start to present information on new projects, grants, loans, and other forms of institutional support.

Kate Selting Smith, of Washington State University and Skagit County Extension, encourages farmers to apply for USDA support. As she explains, it is not only a language or linguistic barrier, it is the broader idea of tracking and quantifying your growing, which challenges farmers who have never learned to monitor their own farming in this way. "It's not the barrier of just filling out the forms," she comments. "The barrier is also the implementation of it. It's just a different concept, and if you haven't gone through business training ... trying to figure out how to explain it [is hard]."

For undocumented farmers, paperwork creates a more definite obstacle. As I discussed in the introduction to this section, to be a verified business owner and sell produce legally, be it to a third party or directly at a market, one must fill out a variety of forms and provide identifying information. Nathan Harkleroad, the education program manager at ALBA in California, shared the limitations he sees undocumented farmers face in terms of loan and support access. "People are afraid to actively pursue those kinds of services because they don't want to be high on the radar, so they might be reluctant to," remarks Harkleroad. "And then there's certain things they won't qualify for, because they're only available to people who have legal residency."

Ostrom talked about the fears that many immigrant farmers who work with the Small Farms Center in Washington State face as undocumented farmers with regard to paperwork: "We still have a lot of problems with documentation and ICE. ... It is still a constant obstacle and worry, and a challenge—a big challenge you think about every single time you have to fill out a document."

Acknowledging that a lot of local farmers are undocumented, she pointed out some of the structural issues for them entering government offices and accessing resources, such as the USDA or extension. As Ostrom put it, "Especially in the extension offices, [the problem] is that they have their offices in the court office, and they have undocumented people. That is not going to work. ... That's where the county government is. It's the property of the county, so it is logical from an economic standpoint; plenty of the extension offices are in the courthouse."

The fact that extension offices may be located in a government building along with a court house or another government establishment may make economic sense, as she explains, but for undocumented farmers, this will undoubtedly prevent them from ever entering the doors. Such fear has been analyzed by other scholars of immigrant agriculturalists' lives in the United States, as the perception of unsafe spaces for undocumented workers is pervasive in the immigrant community, constantly preventing them from accessing resources from food to health care (Mares, Wolcott-MacCausland, and Mazar 2017; Sexsmith 2017).

This fear is not unfounded, as Don McMoran, the director of Washington State University Skagit County Extension, describes his own concerns and regrets regarding some of the outreach they have done with undocumented farmers. "There was one undocumented [farmer] who was deported a few years ago. I felt kind of responsible because, number one, we didn't check, and number two, we are putting them in the face of our community," McMoran says, "and that puts them kind of out there to be a target in my mind."

Although he continued to state that he was unsure that it was farming that made the farmer vulnerable, he was concerned that by owning his own business, instead of blending in as another worker, that it had made him a target for authorities. Melone, of California FarmLink, concurred that although extending resources to immigrant farmers is essential to their success, he struggles with the fact that when they are discriminated against, they cannot safely stand up for themselves due to fear. As Melone comments, "Helping farmers access resources, as is my day-to-day work, can be a double-edged sword, in my experience. Undocumented and even documented farmers who have gone through the trouble of accessing programs of different sorts, and they feel they haven't been treated fairly, don't feel they have recourse to defend their rights, which feels tragic, criminal." The tragedy he describes is that even when farmers go through the hoops of accessing resources, when they face discrimination based on their identity or assumed identity, it can halt the process of ultimately getting such needed support.

In order to convert from worker to farmer, immigrants must successfully navigate entrenched racial, social, and political borders. Despite discrimination and obstacles related to language, literacy, and documentation status, some immigrant farmers are beating the odds, and in the process, re-creating a new and promising sense of place and home. These multiple forms of displacement underlay their deep commitment to an agrarian profession and livelihood, and quest to carve out a social as well as physical place they can call their own.

Growing Practices, Agrodiversity, and Institutional Resources

If a visitor knows where to look, they might be able to tell an immigrants' field in Virginia from their neighbors' field. In contrast to the monocropped, uniform rows of wheat and corn, which line most of the sides of country highways in this region, the immigrants' fields include huge varieties of produce, each row different from the next. Among the cultivated crops, plants such as purslane (also known as *verdolaga* or pigweed), seen as a common weed by US-born farmers, are left to grow between the rows. Farmers harvest purslane for their Latino/a customers and themselves to consume in soups and stews. Juxtaposing the perfectly managed rows of grain, grown by mid-scale white farmers, and kept meticulously free of wild plants with pest-resistant, genetically modified seeds and regular doses of pesticides, the immigrant farmers' fields show signs of agroecological variety. These growing practices are harder to quantify and monitor by existing standards, and ultimately make it more difficult for immigrant farmers to fit into the boxes created by USDA programs, as discussed above. I pursue the disconnects between alternative and agroecological methods of growing and the state, and the need for more inclusive methods for valuing diverse agricultural systems, more in the conclusion to this chapter.

As I explore in more depth in chapter 5, all farmers interviewed saw starting their own farm as a way to regain independence over their daily lives and labor in the face of their limited material wealth as well as political standing. In contrast to their experiences as farmworkers, they have the ability to choose when to rise, what to plant, and how to pick their crops, as long as they operate a productive farm. Cultivating using practices that reflect their own experience reasserts immigrant farmers' control over their own labor, reflecting the global movement for food sovereignty among farmers. To protect this autonomy, many of the farmers I spoke with shied away from interactions with the state, where they may be subjected to standardizing their practices to match a particular form of farming.

And yet their choice to cultivate diverse cropping systems, which work well for direct markets and reflect their own experiences as farmers before immigration, are not supported by the programs made available to them in USDA regional offices. For example, the NRCS office in Virginia's Northern Neck region offers a cover crop assistance program subsidized through state funds. As the staff from the local office explained, this program is not tailored to the needs of diversified fruit and vegetable farmers:

> I also offer this cover crop program for them. That program is through … it's a state program. But most of them—the cover crop has to stay on the land, between certain planting dates and certain dates that you have to destroy. And that date, the destroyer date is after. Because they start planting around February first; the beginning of February they start discing their land, preparing their land. And that cover crop has to stay on there until the middle of March. And that's not good for vegetable farmers at all because they need that time, they need that land. When it's ready to go, they're ready to go.

Figure 3.2
Diverse summer squash and cucumber varieties grown on a Latino/a farm in Virginia.

When I asked the staff person if the cover crops work better for the grain farmers, she told me, "Yes, I have offered several times. I go out there and just try to push the program. And they say no, it's just not good for them because of the rules and regulations of the cover crop program."

This illustration of poor seasonal fit with available NRCS programs could be equally true for any fruit or vegetable farmer in the region. Yet for immigrant farmers, who have fewer farming options due to their limited access to capital investment, land, and markets, this misalignment reinforces an existing inequality for already-disenfranchised farmers.

In another example, in order to participate in the hoop house program, in addition to being subject to random visits and providing a detailed log of what was planted, how much was spent, and how much profit was made, farmers must plant particular crops according to USDA guidelines. Farmers must prepare and adhere to an operation and maintenance plan, which includes particular instructions as to proper irrigation and planting practices as well as erosion control. This plan has to be reviewed and approved by an NRCS official. While the few farmers who participate in the program did not express frustration at these requirements, others stayed away from government offices because they did not want to have to answer to outside authorities. One farmer who chose to participate in the hoop house program conveyed both gratitude and frustration, saying, "We were planting tomatoes, because they're very particular. They [the USDA] want certain stuff. You can't go ahead and do anything you want with them [the hoop houses]. ... And it's good help. I'm not saying it doesn't help, but we've managed to come so far on our own."

While the farmer appreciates the financial assistance, she also questions if the planting restrictions are worth the support. The requirement for standardization feels like a relinquishment of some part of her agrarian autonomy or the ability to make all farming decisions as she wishes. Even for those who succeed in securing state resources, they seem unsure about the decision to work within certain rules and regulations. Yet it is not only government institutions such as the USDA that expect a certain level of standardization for farmer participation. As I discuss below, markets, even farmers markets, which are meant to benefit small-scale growers with diversified crops, can be challenging places for immigrant farmers to enter and gain acceptance.

Market Discrimination

Farmers markets provide farmers with the most direct link to consumers as well as spaces where they can network and socialize with other farmers and food providers. Markets are also generally supportive for farmers who grow diverse crops at varying scales and want to avoid losing profit to intermediary purchasers. Farmers markets should be the ideal outlet for immigrant farmers, who grow a variety of crops in relatively small amounts, and due to language and literacy restrictions, struggle when working with more bureaucratic institutions. Yet like other institutional agrarian spaces in the United States, they often reinforce opportunities for farmers with privilege, while leaving out new farmers of color.

Despite challenges to entry, access, and cultural acceptance, farmers markets were still the most commonly cited places that farmers I met sell their produce. It is in farmers markets where I was first introduced to many of the farmers I later visited and interviewed. Immigrant farmers recounted how these open-air spaces, filled with dozens of produce, meat, bakery, beverage, and prepared-food vendors, were reminiscent of markets where they sold and shopped back in Mexico, providing a familiarity and sense of home, which I explore more in chapter 4. Such markets allow many of them an opportunity to directly meet customers as well as market unique and diverse crops in small quantities. Throughout this research, I spoke to farmers about their experiences selling in markets, and to market managers, other nonimmigrant farmers who sold alongside them, and a few middlepersons, companies, and farmers that rented cooler space for farmers who sell wholesale.

As I mentioned in the introduction to this chapter, many scholars have found that farmers markets can be exclusionary to people of color, as their participants consist of well-connected communities of white farmers and consumers (Alkon and McCullen 2011; Slocum 2007). Such research is unsurprising given my own findings, where market managers are often aware of the cultural expectations of primarily white consumers, and even when they are sympathetic to the needs of immigrant farmers, emphasized the ways that farmers of color can make their own practices more amenable to such consumers. In the section that follows, I discuss multiple ways that immigrant farmers are de-prioritized and forced to struggle in the context of the growing farmers market movement, including gaining entrance and meeting market regulations, and ultimately what it means when they look for alternative routes through wholesale vendors.

Gaining Entrance to Farming Communities

Although many farmers were generally content with their experience selling at farmers markets, others, especially those on the West Coast, struggled to gain entrance. In California in particular, markets are notoriously saturated in large cities, where the customer base is able to spend more money, creating an increasingly profitable venture for farmers. Many immigrant farmers simply cannot gain entry to the most profitable markets due to market saturation. Farmers with spots at these markets tend to be part of a network of farmers with a longer history of selling in the region or that offer something new that customers have not seen before. Typically, vendor spots for farmers with fresh, diverse produce are already filled, mostly with white farmers who have held these spaces for decades. In places where the competition to entry is less stiff and immigrant farmers were successfully selling, I heard stories of blatant discrimination from white farmers, who seemingly felt threatened by the presence of farmworkers turned farmers. White farmers are oftentimes part of communities made up of multiple generations of established farming families. While they may be open to immigrants coming to their regions to perform much-needed labor on their farms, some are uncomfortable seeing them move up the ranks to farm ownership, as is evidenced in the stories told by farmers below.

I drove an hour and a half from Saint Paul to visit Samuel's farm, passing dozens of small lakes and worn-looking red barns nestled among hilly green pastures. Samuel, a farmer of mixed vegetables, is a leader in the immigrant farming community in Minnesota. He works not only on his own farm but is also as an adviser for other farmers through the Latino Economic Development Center in the Twin Cities. Samuel explains that "it's very difficult to be in a market that has been controlled by whites for generations. All of a sudden to show up as Latino, with this face ... is very difficult." As Samuel makes clear, as immigrants of color, he and his fellow farmers stand out from the other vendors, and they are aware of their social difference as they try to connect with consumers and other farmers at markets.

Beyond institutional forms of discrimination, farmers told stories of individual racialized aggressions by other farmers and customers, thereby constraining their potential profitability and business growth. Farmers often feel unwelcome in the primarily white farming community. In the 1980s, Jesus was one of the first immigrant orchardists in Washington State. He came from Mexico to work in the orchards, with barely a grade school education and no ability to speak English. He now owns dozens of acres and has been farming in the same community for over thirty years. Jesus told me that "there are farmers who have to spend years fighting preconceived notions of Latino farmers. Once they see that you are just another guy with a family and kids, and they see that you participate in sports and everything, just like the next guy. With a little bit of time, you get accepted in the community."

He was positive about the transition to a more inclusive environment for immigrants in his region. In his community, immigrant farmers have been establishing themselves for several decades. In other immigrant farming communities where they are less familiar to their neighbors, I heard less positive stories. Gerardo started farming when he was seven years old with his grandfather in Oaxaca, Mexico. He came to the United States when he was twelve years old with his family. He has owned his own farm in California for the past two years. Unique among my research participants, Gerardo has a college degree. Despite his formal education, he still feels that other farmers do not take him seriously. When asked about how other farmers in his community treat him, Gerardo put it this way, "There will be people who will put you down, but what is more important is if you let them push you down. Because they will look at you like, 'I'm better than you.' A lot of people will say, 'He is this or he is that because we are not from the same race.'"

Although he takes personal responsibility for overcoming such prejudice, others were more forthright in the challenges such preconceived notions created for them. Martin, who farms in Virginia and was introduced earlier, stated that his previous employers were angry when they learned he was starting his own farm. He had managed their farm for twenty-seven years, yet they were not supportive of his transition and started talking badly about him to other farmers. He began selling his own produce at the same market where he had sold on behalf of his white employers for almost thirty years. He only did so after his former employers decided to stop going to the market and focus on wholesale. He found the other vendors were not tolerant of a Mexican farmer selling his own produce at the market.[10] Two white farmers tried to get him ousted from the market—an act that he believes was motivated by jealousy and racial discrimination:

> I have had clients there for twenty-five, thirty years. Regularly, for years, they have bought from me [when I was selling for my former employer]. I bring two hundred, three hundred watermelons in the truck and I sell them all. [The other vendors] brought seventy, and they couldn't sell them. It made them mad, and they wanted me kicked out. The next year, two white women tried to get me expelled because I sold a lot. So the people [my customers] started to help me, so they couldn't run me out.

Of course, entrepreneurs do not typically cheer on their competition. At the markets where these farmers sell, there are dozens of farmers selling at a range of prices. Immigrants do not stand out as the lowest sellers or particularly different than the other vendors—other than their race and nationality, and somewhat-larger variety of produce, with some additional Latin American varieties. In the case of immigrant farmers, the negative reactions are rooted in a suspicion of outsiders in a white farm-operator community. A university extension agent in Virginia affirmed this type of discrimination against "newcomers," entrenched in a general mistrust of a new group of farmers they do not know. "They're good growers, and I think, pretty successful," notes this agent. "And I think that can cause other farmers to be jealous. Not necessarily in the area, but across the board at a market. And I think a lot of fingers get pointed. And I think that the things that people say they do. ... The biggest thing a lot of times is that there's mistrust, in terms of if they're actually growing what they saying they're growing; that's probably the biggest."

Arguably, "jealousy" of new, nonwhite farmers is related to the fact that white farmers are used to immigrants working for rather than selling alongside them. It therefore makes sense that some would feel threatened and reactive to Latino/a farmers' class advancements. The sense that white farmers are somehow threatened or experiencing a disadvantage, as compared to immigrant farmers, is a trend observed by Melone, with California FarmLink, as well. "Over the years I've heard complaints from established white farmers, that farmers who participate in incubator and training programs, and have people advocating on their behalf, are getting land at reduced rates and unfair advantages," explains Melone. "Meanwhile, these same people don't acknowledge the family support they received in starting their farm, accessing markets, inheriting their land, etc."

As Melone points out, while established farmers focus on the resources, limited as they are, being allocated to immigrant farmers, they are disregarding their own advantages, such as inherited land and family support. Further, as I discuss below, white farmers tend to be given the benefit of the doubt regarding their marketing and growing practices, while immigrant farmers are more likely to be targeted for violating market rules, not only by other farmers who might feel economically threatened, but by seemingly neutral market managers.

Discrimination through Market Regulation

Another way immigrant farmers are held back from success in local markets is through farmers market regulations. The agent quoted above is referencing the requirement at most farmers markets for vendors to only sell what they grow, not resell from other farmers, stores, or brokers. Although requirements are not standardized across states, regions, or market organizations, markets regularly have regional or distance-based requirements to ensure products are being produced on a local scale. The umbrella organizations that manage markets are usually nonprofit groups, overseeing multiple markets in one region. Many of them have market managers who conduct site visits and check that producers are actually growing what they sell.

Immigrant farmers cited stories of direct discrimination by markets managers. A farmer in Virginia, Bertha, who is originally from Oaxaca, described racialized targeting by market managers unequivocally: "Even if they [my customers] point the finger at the gringos, they come inspect the Hispanics. Even if they're the clients who are complaining, they all come the same. ... So if someone complains about a gringo, they come inspect us. And they say that the gringos have everything [in order], and to all of us, they give us a paper to see if we have everything [that we say we have]. We know it's all lies, but what are we going to do? ... Yes, especially if it's a gringo [complaining], they only inspect the Hispanics."

Although most white farmers are honestly growing and selling from their own farms, they are also more likely to be given the benefit of the doubt than immigrant farmers. Adam Sanders, an immigrant and refugee

Figure 3.3
Diverse crops sold by a Latino/a farmer at a farmers market in Washington State.

advocate, was my initial connection to many of the farmers I interviewed in California. He worked closely with a group of Triqui farmworkers (indigenous to Mexico) on the Central Coast of California to help them start a community garden to ensure their food security. Sanders later assisted many of them through the bureaucracy of starting their own farms and accessing markets. He worked as a broker for many of them, bringing their produce to the city to connect them with markets, as they did not speak English or have access to long-distance transportation. He also explained the ways that more established white farmers seemed to break the rules. Through their many years of market experience, Sanders said, white farmers were able to gain further advantages by repackaging other growers' produce:

> You get these bigger farms with these big tables and all this beautiful variety, and if they're buying well over half that stuff from small farmers, it doesn't represent the true cost. If they were growing that themselves, their profit would not be as high, and so that's how they're getting money and profitability. And when other people were coming in and selling their own stuff. ... But most people do it, the bigger stands do it, and people don't realize that. I saw it from the inside, and it's really disappointing.

While I cannot verify that this is standard practice, Sanders is making an important point that when white farmers break rules, they are assumed innocent, while immigrant farmers are assumed guilty, reflecting the observations made by immigrant farmers themselves.

In my many meetings with farmers market managers who work at markets heavily populated by immigrant farmers, they expressed frustration in their efforts to ensure that all farmers abide by market rules. They recognize that misunderstandings are common, yet in my interviews, even well-intentioned managers reinforced farmers' suspicions that they oftentimes assumed that newcomers to the market were less likely to follow market regulations. Most did not speak fluent Spanish themselves, and had to communicate through farmers' children or other translators, when available. Due to linguistic and cultural barriers, they were unable to communicate directly with many immigrant farmers, and therefore unable to ask detailed or difficult questions about their growing practices. Likewise, because of these barriers, farmers were not given equal opportunities to explain their products. Most managers spoke with me about this divide, and the ways they were actively trying to bridge gaps in communication and education. Examples include having regulations for farmers translated into Spanish as well as helping immigrant farmers with signage and other forms of advertising.

Ostrom, from Washington State extension, works directly with market managers. Much of her work focuses on helping managers become more culturally sensitive so as to bridge the linguistic divide between managers and farmers, and make markets more generally accessible to immigrant farmers. Yet she recognizes these divides are still common, and thinks they lead to regular miscommunications and misunderstandings between market managers and immigrant farmers. "Even the farmers markets, how do managers treat people there?" Ostrom asks. "I feel like they're not getting along. Is it because the farmers are mostly trying not to follow rules? Or they're just not understanding each other?"

While it may be a point of miscommunication between immigrant farmers and nonimmigrant managers, this does not dispel the fact that managers unfairly assume that immigrants are breaking market rules, particularly that of bringing in produce they did not grow themselves. This suspicion on the part of managers is directly related to the fact that markets are predominantly populated by white vendors and customers, creating a sense that nonwhite farmers are out of place. Market managers were open in addressing farmers' inequalities, but most have a long way to go to face their racial bias head-on. In the meantime, immigrant farmers are being put to more stringent tests to stay active in markets and under more pressure to prove their legitimacy in the eyes of market authorities.

Other Market Options

Despite all their best intentions, many immigrant farmers are not able to economically survive the farmers market competition. The most lucrative farmers markets are saturated with mixed-crop and vegetable growers, and will not take in more vendors with similar products. Some farmers who started out growing more diverse crops for direct markets have had to switch to less diverse wholesale production after struggling to gain entry to farmers markets already saturated with vegetable growers. To sell to larger wholesale distributors, farmers have to grow a more consistent amount of fewer products. In order to make a profit at selling a few crops to wholesalers versus a diversity to direct markets, scaling up becomes an imperative. In California in particular, many immigrant farmers were working on breaking into wholesale markets, including selling to third-party brokers as well as other direct markets, such as restaurants and retailers. These kinds of markets present their own challenges for immigrant farmers. Some of these are standard to any farmer selling wholesale, such as the cost of storage and large-scale coolers, and the lost profit to middlepersons. Wholesalers expect a consistent quality and large quantity, in contrast to farmers market consumers who are generally more content with less consistent and uniform crops, and are willing to pay more for local and certified organic or sustainably grown produce.

Yet for some, reducing diversity and scaling up has been their only option. Even farmers in regions with easier entry to direct markets were finding it difficult to sell all the produce they grew. Markets were the most commonly cited limiting factor to their farm businesses' survival.

For new immigrant farmers, those who are struggling to adjust to a new culture, the aggressive and competitive marketing necessary to secure high-end customers outside farmers markets is beyond what they are able to successfully take on. Sanders, who spent a year brokering produce for mostly indigenous immigrant farmers, saw culture as an almost-larger boundary than language:

Who's able to actually make the money are those people who are willing to break out of the shadows. And there are a few of them, but it's hard. ... And a lot of it, especially in the Oaxacan culture, is the politeness. And in produce, I found out you've got to be calling people on the phone, and if someone's yelling at somebody else, you've got to yell back at them. You've got to push; you've got to send pictures constantly and know what the prices are every day. So it's not even an English thing. There are a lot of people born and raised here who speak English and couldn't do it. It's highly stressful to do wholesale produce.

Just as with farmers markets, of course, the farmers must leave the farm and drive many hours to bring their produce to customers. For many, especially those who are undocumented, travel can be intimidating. Additionally, for many immigrant farmers, the attraction to farming is the connection to the land itself; regardless of documentation status, they would prefer to stay home and not to travel.[11] Sanders elaborates: "But it's the fear of driving, the need of connecting with the farm. ... And what we had wanted to do was—I offered many, many times to cross-train people and invited them to drive with me on my route, especially the kids. ... But in some families, there's this hesitation to do that, and they just want to be on the farm."

Despite these structural challenges, some farmers, even recent immigrants with no formal education, overcome cultural barriers and fear. As I
have shown throughout the book, what immigrant farmers all share is their
resilience and ability to overcome extreme barriers to creating a landed life
in the United States. Against all odds, they are continuously proving their
skills and commitment, and fulfilling their dreams of an agrarian livelihood. Sanders describes one of the more successful farmers he worked with
in California:

> Part of it was his partner who pushes him, and she says, "Look, I'm not afraid to
> be calling people; you're great at farming. You take care of the farming, and I'll
> do this." But see, before he'd even finished ALBA, he got his labels, he got them
> [organically] certified by CCOF. He got his food safety certification. He made
> these big beautiful labels he put on everything with all the correct information,
> kept it updated according to the laws, which you know changed, and now you
> have to put more information on your sticker. ... He would ask the questions and
> push. And they're not afraid to go to a printer in Watsonville, and walk in the
> door and say, "I need you to make me ten thousand of these." They're not afraid
> to do that.

As Sanders makes clear, the boundaries to enter markets for immigrant
growers are high, but not impossible to overcome. Not only do they need
to face overt racial discrimination, the related challenges of language and
culture create more subtle challenges as they work to develop a customer
base. Further, as farmers trying to enter both wholesale and direct markets,
many immigrants struggle with attracting and connecting with customers.
It is an additional challenge to market their businesses, as they lack the
linguistic and technological skills to brand their farms and garner attention
on the same level as white-owned, direct-market farms. Famers who are
able to market their products successfully tend to have entered the United
States at a younger age, or have US-raised children who are fluent in English
and more immersed in US culture. These farmers can more easily engage in
social media and branding schemes. It is easier for them to have attractive
and accurate signage and business cards at the markets as well as post reci-
pes and promotions online. While several of the farms excelled at this kind
of promotion, most lacked the human resources and experience, struggling
to foster a client base and branding in order to stand out among the other
farms in their region.

In both farmers markets and wholesale, their differences as immigrants and farmers of color become clear as they struggle with acceptance from other farmers as well as marketing their business in spaces where they are treated suspiciously and without merit. In farming communities and food spaces, which are defined as default color-blind places, whiteness acts as a boundary, keeping farmers from being accepted, and being given preference or the benefit of the doubt when compared with other farmers. These boundaries keep immigrant farmers from advancing economically, maintaining agrarian ethnic and racial disparities.

Organic Certification

Similar to regulations and standards at farmers markets, the organic label, possibly the most well-recognized qualification for alternative farmers, can be a barrier for immigrant farmers gaining access to the full economic benefits of their growing practices. As I have mentioned in other chapters, most of the immigrant farmers I interviewed grow using minimal or no synthetic additives, and have experience with practices such as composting and building soil as well as other farming practices considered as "sustainable." Yet many are not certified as organic. Several who are not certified expressed interest in the process, but do not have the resources to pay for the certification process or are intimidated by the paperwork involved, and thus are not able to advertise as "certified organic." For those who do not own all the land they are growing on, it is difficult to confirm that the land has not been cultivated using synthetic additives in recent years—a requirement for certification. Furthermore, they do not want to invest in improving land where they are unsure of their tenure.

Julie Guthman (2014) discusses the institutional and racialized boundaries to organic certification in her book *Agrarian Dreams: The Paradox of Organic Farming in California*. She looks at the history of organic certification as it reflects the broader history of stronger institutional and government support for white farmers as well as those with more land and resources. Guthman argues that standardizing and the scientification of certification benefits larger and more industrial-style farmers, rather than smaller-scale and more diverse, resource-poor farmers, such as farmers of color. Additionally, she explains that since smaller-scale farmers, who are selling primarily to direct markets, have more contact with consumers, they have less incentive to prove they are organic and therefore less motivation for certification than larger-scale farmers.

I heard over and over again from farmers that getting certified is costly and less optimal for those who rent their farmland, since the certification of the land takes three years and cannot be transferred by a farmer to another property. As soil building without synthetic additives requires more labor, it is also an investment in the future of the property—again, not a wise economic decision for renters, who may or may not stay on the land after the process is complete.

Some farmers recognized the advantage of certification, but discussed the paperwork and lack of literacy as their primary boundary. Manuel, who is from Oaxaca, learned how to farm from his parents and has little formal education. He currently farms in the state of Washington. It was clear that not having certification was not for lack of interest but rather a lack of funds and the ability to fill out the paperwork. "I would like to do it. ... I think that by registering as organic, more doors will open," says Manuel. "They can't just buy your product because they don't know how you're growing. I tell my daughters to help me [with the paperwork for certification], but they are focused on their studies."

Many farmers acknowledged that they are already doing the extra labor of organic farming, yet they cannot justify the expense and time to do the paperwork. Marisela works on a certified organic farm in Washington State during the day as a laborer and comes back to work with her husband in the evenings on their own rented land. She knows what organic certification takes and believes in its value, but they cannot afford to go through the process. She told me, "It is better to be organic, but at the same time is more paperwork and is another expense." Ricardo, introduced above, simply said, "We looked into it. Money is the issue."

In the context of farmer discrimination and opportunity, organic certification is another way that institutional structures prevent immigrant farmers from receiving the same benefits as more established, larger-scale, or US-born farmers. Organic certification, for better or worse, has become the nationally and universally recognized standard for how the average consumer identifies sustainable farming. When immigrant farmers cannot access the advantage of marketing themselves as such, they lose out on potential revenue and advancement.

Toward a New Era of Inclusion

In this chapter, I review both the structural and individual ways that immigrant farmers are left behind in accessing institutional resources and networks. From the federal government to neighborhood farmers markets, Latino/a immigrant farmers are not extended the same opportunities as white farmers. This inequality only furthers the existing divides in capital, markets, and land necessary for farmers to survive in today's increasingly competitive agricultural economy.

As I have discussed, the USDA is the headquarters for claims of discrimination as well as the most appropriate location for overcoming structural racial injustice. Although the USDA is not the only institutional boundary for Latino/a immigrant farmers, nor the only place improvements can and should be made, it is the only state institution that claims to provide economic opportunities for rural communities and agricultural producers of the United States. While there are many entrepreneurial and nonprofit ventures that focus on advancement for and training of small farmers, farmers of color, and immigrant farmers, those are often working on shoestring budgets, with varying levels of accountability to their clients, and have limited access to resources and markets themselves. The USDA supports many of these projects, including farmers markets and organic certification groups, through grants and other institutional backing; therefore addressing structural discrimination at the USDA must be a focus of improvement if services are going to reach farmers of all racial and ethnic backgrounds in a just manner.

Under Vilsack's guidance, the USDA took several steps toward a new vision of equality at the federal level. From 2009 until 2016, it provided civil rights trainings to employees, established the Office of Advocacy and Outreach to aid beginning and socially disadvantaged farmers, and claimed to work toward resolving civil rights lawsuits inherited from previous administrations. The department vowed to be an equal opportunity employer and create a workforce that "represents the full diversity of America" (USDA-OASCR 2015).

This was all under the Obama administration. As I was completing the fieldwork for this project, Trump was elected president, and Sonny Perdue, an agribusiness executive who took a strong anti-immigrant stance as the governor of Georgia, was sworn in as the secretary of agriculture. On a national level, we are seeing massive cuts in government spending, which on a regional and local scale means further cuts in funding to extension, grants, staff, and staff trainings, such as those that could be used to improve the racial exclusion of immigrant farmers from institutions, opportunities, and programs. While it is too early to know exactly how such reforms under the new administration will unfold for farmers exactly, projections do not look good. After the election, I attempted to follow up with staff at the USDA inquiring about what they thought the new administration would mean for immigrants and other farmers of color. Requests for feedback were either declined or not answered. While my inquiry was not exhaustive, I can imagine most staff still employed by the USDA are not looking to critique the administration from their current positions.

Unfortunately, even during the previous administration, I found that despite claims of increased racial equality from the federal offices of the USDA, little change was being made on the ground in local and regional offices to directly help Latino/a immigrants overcome obstacles in order to transition from the role of farmworker to farmer in the United States. The processes of monitoring and standardization, as currently required by USDA programs, exacerbate the racial exclusion of immigrant farmers from state programs and, ultimately, the advantages that other farmers receive. This uneven rural development must be understood in the context of the historical relationship between immigrants and the state as well as the lived experiences of those struggling within a system where their practices are not deemed readable. Today's immigrant farmers follow this pattern of racialized others being left out of a system where some practices are deemed legible and thus legitimate, and others are not. If anything, change has gone in the wrong direction. Government programs have the potential to provide wraparound services that could include immigrant farmers in planning, markets, and other institutions, which could potentially benefit them, but such programs are chronically underfunded and currently having their budget further decimated.

In recent years, and as a result of the lawsuits mentioned above, the USDA has devoted new funding to support farmers identified as socially disadvantaged, such as minority farmers, Latino/a farmers included. As previously mentioned, programs that are developed for the specific needs of diversified fruit and vegetable or specialty crop growers already exist within the USDA. The FSA also offers microloan programs designed for "nontraditional" farmers that require less paperwork and could be helpful for Latino/a immigrants as they transition to farm ownership. Additionally, the Minority and Socially Disadvantaged Farmers Assistance office has been established within the FSA with the express purpose of assisting farmers such as those who participated in this study. Despite critique, many of the farmers described in this book have indirectly benefited from the support of local and direct-market initiatives funded by the agency. These programs are a great start to making government-supported programs available to immigrant growers. Regrettably, due to social divides along with language and educational barriers, these programs are unknown to those most in need of assistance.

Further, programs that support new and beginning farmers as well as organic and direct-market programs are only funded through temporary measures. Even more established and bipartisan programs are vulnerable to political swings, especially in our current political moment, as they require reinstatement by the Farm Bill.

Of course, some paperwork and state monitoring are necessary for programs to function and farmers to be held accountable. I do not suggest that these procedures can or should be simply abolished. Rather, these processes must be streamlined to take account of differences in growing practices, linguistic and literacy capabilities, and the need for farmers to maintain autonomy on multiple levels, if they are to build the trust that is so sorely lacking. Programs should be amended to account for differential growing seasons for diverse crops. While not a structural or universally beneficial fix, technologies such as camera phones could be better utilized for documentation purposes in contrast to lengthy written paperwork—an idea suggested to me by Marie Ullrich, a Vegetable Specialist with Cornell Cooperative Extension in New York. In all my discussions with USDA and other outreach staff members, there was an interest in these changes being made to accommodate "nontraditional" farmers in the United States.

Specifically, mainstream agricultural research and education models that are not appropriate for many immigrant farmers, who lack may formal education and English skills, and who also may not be farming using conventional or industrial methods, need to be adjusted to meet farmers where they are (Ostrom, Cha, and Flores 2010; Rovegno 2016). Various institutions like Washington State University's Small Farms Program and Virginia Tech's extension services in the Northern Neck have partnered

Figure 3.4
Posters in English and Spanish advertising a small farmer and rancher training organized by Washington State University's Small Farm Program.

with nonprofits to help enhance their ability to translate, train staff, and develop culturally appropriate educational tools and resources. Examples like these must be replicated and pushed up the chain of command within the federal offices and with decision makers. It is in these programs that the disconnects between the state's expectation of conventional growing and white farming culture and alternative, agroecological, and nonwhite practices and cultures are being addressed. There is an enormous need for more inclusive methods and approaches such as these in order to properly value as well as support diverse agricultural systems.

Immigrant farmers are challenging historical racial legacies in farming in the United States, despite the odds, and persisting in new markets and climates that are seemingly unattainable. The USDA has the opportunity to support their growth as farmers, but in order for programs and funding to reach the most financially disadvantaged beginning farmers, the agency must do more to recognize the challenges that immigrant farmers experience in the current system. A productive first step in addressing the long-standing fear of state authority is certainly the recognition of its existence, yet more must be done to truly make services and financial support available. To start with, USDA staff in local offices need better support for linguistic and cultural translations, and outreach must focus on making farmers feel safe and included. This support must be available consistently throughout the United States, and not just in offices where farmers are already participating. For this to happen, awareness must improve more broadly at the national level where decisions are made, such as in the Farm Bill debates. Individuals at the local level are powerless if federal leadership does not make concrete changes to procedures and funding streams to support these changes. To truly transition to a new age of civil rights, political leadership and leadership at the USDA must look closely at local conditions and challenges that individual groups of socially disadvantaged farmers face, and make clear and grounded changes to include them.

This chapter highlights immigrant farmer encounters with institutional and individual discrimination, which for many is a day-to-day struggle. These experiences mark immigrant farmers' class transition from worker to owner as deeply embedded in racial and citizenship-based politics. Despite these struggles, they continue to progress in challenging agrarian social hierarchies. In the following chapters, I explore what motivates immigrant farmworkers to persist in their quest for farm ownership, the forms that their farms take, and the specific practices that they choose to employ.

4 Food, Identity, and Agricultural Practice: Re-creating Home through the Family Farm

It's part of our heritage that we want to be able to not have to ... get up at a certain time, but not just jump in a car and leave your house. It's more a way of life, being able to raise your kids at home, because everybody where we're from has their own farm. Every single person in town had their own farm.
—Carlos

Carlos and Lorena came to the United States from Michoacán in search of better job opportunities. The couple rents eight acres on which they farm mixed vegetables and own a house a few miles from the farm site. They came to upstate New York to work in the vineyards, pruning and harvesting in the newly burgeoning wine industry of the Finger Lakes region.[1] As he explains above, once Carlos was settled in the United States, he wanted to re-create something that reminded him of his life back home in Mexico. He described a place where his family could work and eat homegrown food together, and his children could learn about the value of an agrarian livelihood. When the couple had saved enough money, they began to cultivate their rented land in the evenings after working all day in the vineyards. After almost ten years, they were able to quit their day jobs and commit to their own farm full time.[2]

In this chapter, I tell the story of people moving across borders, and the practices and land-based identities that travel with them. Most of the farmers interviewed for this book expressed a desire to farm in a way that helped them develop a sense of place or home in the United States. Key to that home is space where they can produce food to feed their families in a safe and healthy manner, and teach their children about food-growing practices and culture. Farming enables immigrant farmers to re-create a way of life similar to the one they had in Mexico, grounded in food and family. Farmers articulated an aspiration to maintain a smaller-scale, less intensive farming style, and remain living on or near the land they cultivate. In many ways, this vision contrasts with the industrial farms they have worked on as hired laborers and instead resembles the farms they remembered from their own childhoods.

As many immigrants explained, they farm in the United States in part to re-create a *recuerdo*, or memory, of their former lifestyle in Mexico. These agricultural spaces are representative of a desire for re-creating a home place, where farmers are able to define their own livelihoods and spaces. Further, creating these spaces provides them an opportunity to find a way to belong and feel permanence in a country where many have been migrating as seasonal laborers for decades. Particularly in today's political climate, which can feel threatening for immigrants, connecting their experience from their country of origin to their new home in the United States can create a sense of safety and permanence.

Figure 4.1
Carlos and Lorena Aguilera of Summer Times Farm at their home in New York State.

As many scholars have noted, re-creating food and agricultural practices from home countries often enables immigrants in the United States to maintain land- and food-based identities and cultural traditions as they cross spatial and political boundaries (Abarca 2006; Mares 2012; Mares and Peña 2010; Peña 2005). Yet as Doreen Massey (1994) points out, although capital and the relatively recent process of globalization force people to forge a new sense of home geographically, for many, especially those from the colonized world, "home" has never been constant. Dislocation and reorganization of a sense of home, in terms of social relations and one's identity concerning home, are never fixed. Similarly, Stuart Hall (1990) contends that the cultural identity of diasporic peoples must always be understood as hybrid, through the process of transformation and change, rather than stuck in an essentialized notion of home. The immigrant farmers discussed in this book are reclaiming agricultural practices as a way of creating a new sense of home—one building on past experiences of landedness, but entrenched in new relations with state power as well as a landscape already occupied by white farmers.

Today's immigrant workers turned farmers are unique in the context of global agrarian change, finding ways to maintain small-scale family operated farms by combining subsistence-based practices and farming styles acquired in Mexico with those learned by working on farms in the United States. Their motivation to farm is rooted in their agrarian identities; they see farming as a way to both revive their past and create a new future. This fluid use of geographically and culturally merged practices can be contextualized in Jeffrey Pilcher's (1996, 1998) work, where he argues that the relationship between food and Mexican identity is unique in that it is a blend of indigenous and Spanish cuisines and influences, representing a deep mixing of cultural and racial identities over time. Drawing on her own familial experience with cross-border Mexican foodways, Meredith Abarca (2017, 39) introduces the notion of "culinary subjectivities," whereby people's food choices and related practices are defined by taste, which "links us to migratory histories of people who have been responsible for establishing certain foodstuffs as supplementary to our diets." These processes and food-related identities, she argues, are constantly renegotiated through culture, society, and history, and are not bound by place and time. Similarly, Teresa Mares, Naomi Wolcott-MacCausland, and Jessie Mazar (2017) as well as Tanachi Pandoongpatt (2017) tell stories of immigrants using foodways to reclaim a sense of place and self when immersed in a new country and culture, where much of their former livelihoods have been lost. In this chapter, I build on and engage with these complex notions of migration, food, practice, and identity, analyzing the difference that social, political, and cultural borders make for redeveloping a land-based home.

While farming practices are often a fusion of experiences acquired in their home countries with those learned in the United States, immigrant farmers lean toward farming approaches that could be easily identified with national and global alternative farming movements, including small-scale and biodiverse plots, low synthetic inputs, direct marketing, family participation, and specialized products from their home country. Of course, small-scale, diverse, and low-input farming practices are also common among white and nonimmigrant farmers, particularly those who identify with the growing alternative food and food sovereignty movements. As has been well documented, many farmers across the world choose to farm using more ecologically and community-based practices for ethical reasons, even to the detriment of their bottom line (see Barham 1997; McMichael 2013; van der Ploeg 2013), as I discuss more in chapter 5. The difference is that for Latino/a immigrant farmers, they are not necessarily choosing these practices due to a connection to global social movements but rather are driven by their cross-cultural identities and experiences as immigrants and small-scale farmers in Mexico.[3]

Those interviewed see farming as a way of life. It is an opportunity to utilize recently acquired as well as home-based knowledge to operate their own business, feed their family, and reconstruct a sense of home lost through migration. Returning to farming reinforces their land-based identities, connecting them to their previous lives, while also allowing them a new chance to establish autonomy in the global agricultural system. They recognize that they are making choices that are not always economically advantageous, including the initial decision to farm. Their practices are related to their limited scale and scope of production, as has been discussed throughout the book, but they are not simply a matter of constraints. In contrast, in this chapter I highlight the ways in which they are motivated by their goal to maintain a family centered, agrarian lifestyle—one that is reminiscent of their daily customs and routines in their countries of origin.

Leaving the Land, Taking What They Know

Sergio has a wide grin and wears a black cowboy hat. In his early twenties, he was one of the younger farmers I interviewed. Sergio grew up farming in Honduras, one of the few farmers in this study who was not born in Mexico. When he arrived in the United States, he got his first job as a construction worker in Arizona, but struggled to adapt to an urban lifestyle. He eventually moved to the Yakima Valley in Washington, where he fell in love with the agrarian landscape. "This is my thing," he told me. "It's like where I came from. This is my life." He travels about four hours two times per week to sell in farmers markets in the greater Seattle area. Although he struggles to make ends meet, compared to his parents' life in Honduras, he sees much potential in farming in the United States. "My parents live in a lot of poverty. It's very stressful to plant corn and beans; that's what we usually grow. We grow vegetables, but not as a business [in Honduras]. Right now, we live off the coffee. Beans and corn are difficult to grow, so my parents live off what the land gives them."

Sergio, and others interviewed for this book, came to the United States as part of the mass exodus of former smallholders and peasants from Central America and Mexico who make up the underpaid, largely undocumented labor force working in US fields today. Although he acknowledges that it is different farming in the United States as compared with his home country, his choice to stay in agriculture is largely based on experiences from his youth. When asked why he decided to pursue agriculture as a business, he told me, "Because it's what we know, it's how we grew up, it's what we know how to do. ... There is a tendency to do what you know how to do as opposed to risk it with something that you don't know. If you don't have the experience and the capacity, then it's more complicated."

Many farmers described their farms as a way to return to the lifestyle or place they remember before emigrating. In interviews, farmers would regularly explain that farming is simply their way of being and what they have always known. Adelso, like other farmers, told me, "I just wanted to be a farmer. I like to grow fruit, I've been doing it all of my life." Or Marisela, who said, "Where I grew up, my grandfather and father grew corn and grains, so that's what we are doing." It was a clear connection for them, continuing their family traditions and using the agrarian knowledge that had been handed down to them from their own parents.

Ernesto is originally from Puebla, Mexico. He has been in the United States twenty-five years and owns a farm in the Hudson Valley. He grows a variety of vegetables, which he sells at farmers markets in New York City. Ernesto describes farming as a *"Recuerdo* [memory] from Mexico. ... We grew up in Mexico, in the country, from generation to generation." He sees farming as an extension of his former life across the border and a way to connect his past with his present.

Saul comes from an agricultural background in Mexico, but for over thirteen years has been living in California, where he now owns and operates a certified organic farm. He made a similar statement regarding his family history of farming, and how the practices of growing food connects him to his culture and way of life in his former home. Saul told me, "I come from the country in Michoacán. We are agricultural workers by nature. I don't know if this has happened to you, but when you see a plant you wonder, 'How does it grow? Can I have it in my garden?' I mean, you have that instinct to grow something and produce it. We grow a lot of corn over there. That is part of my culture, I think."

Saul sees farming as a part of who he is, no matter where he is geographically located. For him, it is part of his identity, culture, and way of knowing the world. But for farmers like Saul, it is not enough to simply have a place to grow food. Farming is about a way of life, an agrarian culture. To live and farm in the same place is a goal for all the immigrant farmers I interviewed. It is important to them to raise their children on a homestead and teach them to grow food, as most of them were taught in Mexico. Unfortunately, in regions like New York's Hudson Valley and California's Central Coast, land prices are too high to consider landownership, although some had succeeded at renting a house on or near where they farm. In the Northern Neck of Virginia, in contrast to other regions, land prices are reasonably affordable, and almost all the farmers had bought land with an established home on the property or are currently working toward building a home on their land.

Catalina, a farmer in Virginia, achieved the dream of living on her own land. She specializes in cut flowers and mixed herbs, and owns her farm, which includes a home garden and a small house on the land, where she lives with her children and husband. Serving me coffee in her living room, she paused to look out the window across her beautifully cultivated fields, with dozens of colorful flower varieties in bloom. She told me that she found life in the United States "very, very ugly. ... Each person stays in their own house. There is no time. People live by their watch, and there is a lot of stress." In contrast, on her farm, "It is a little bit like Mexico. It makes me feel the same. It is not the same exactly, but more free. In the city, there is more pressure." She explained that on her farm, she grows the crop varieties she liked to eat in Mexico and spends her days cultivating food for her family, which all make her feel closer to her home and family she left in Jalisco.

Like Catalina, Mateo, a farmer who grows mixed vegetables in California, reminisced about Mexico and lamented the fact that he could not afford to own land in the United States as part of his agrarian vision. He told me, "It is more peaceful there. Here, the lifestyle is faster. We don't have a house on our ranch here. In Mexico, we do. I'd like to live on a house on the ranch, but here, it is too expensive to buy." In California, where land prices are steep, most farmers, even those who are born in the United States, do not own the land they farm.

Andy Rea, a former agriculture education program manager at ALBA in California, trained aspiring farmers in the business and practice of organic growing. His farmer training courses included both US- and Mexican-born farmers as well as those from other countries with a range of agricultural backgrounds. I asked him how it was different for aspiring farmers from rural Mexican backgrounds as compared with US-born farmers who might have more financial resources to start. He confirmed what farmers told me themselves: "I like to reassure them when they come into the class that they've got a leg up on others. They have the practical experience. They've worked without chemicals. They know, because they couldn't afford them. Some of them realize they've been doing this for hundreds of years already." As he notes, their rural knowledge and experience with low chemical inputs are their advantages in a competitive agricultural market.

While the cost of land is certainly a huge barrier to realizing their dreams, many still feel their experience farming in the United States is easier than it was for their predecessors in Mexico in terms of their daily labor. Alejandro, mentioned in chapter 3, discussed the challenges of farming in Mexico versus the United States. With little resources to invest in machinery, his family members in Mexico do all their labor by hand. "[We have a farm in] Colima. I have lime, plantain, and coconut. ... It's a little bit different. There are more opportunities here to have machinery and buy everything you want. In Mexico, it's harder; you have to do it all by hand. It's very difficult." In the United States, Alejandro has been able to enter the farmers market circuit in the greater Seattle area, where he can make a decent profit off his produce as compared to what his family makes farming in Mexico. He has been able to buy a tractor, which lessens his physical labor. He views this as a large improvement from the way his family farms in Mexico, and despite other challenges, sees himself settling in the United States with his family.

Like Alejandro, most farmers are clear they want to stay in the United States. Pedro, a farmer in California, explained to me, "I am going back, but only to visit my grandparents. I am going to stay here. We are arranging my wife's papers, so we will be able to leave, but only to visit the family. I like it here." After working for many years to start a successful farm in the United States, Pedro reflects the sentiments of many of the farmers I interviewed: this country is where they have raised their children and have their community, so it is now their home, and they want to stay.

Yet despite their emotional and economic investment in the United States, other farmers still dream of returning to their birth country. Several said they would eventually retire in Mexico once their children had been educated. Sonia is from Jalisco, where she started farming at seven years old. She came to the United States as a young adult, migrating throughout the southern United States as a worker in the berry fields. She eventually settled in Virginia, and started her own farm with her husband and parents. The crops they grow are common staples in a Mexican diet, including tomatillos, tomatoes, zucchini, and corn. She told me, "That is my dream, one day, when my youngest son turns eighteen. I don't want to take the opportunity away from him to study here, but once he is able to be on his own here, I can go back to Mexico."

Regardless of whether they plan to remain in the United States permanently, like most immigrants, many send remittances to their original hometowns. Some mentioned the ways that farming in the United States allows them to help provide for family back home. Victoria is originally from Colima. She had some experience growing food with her father as a child, but after her father passed, Victoria and her family stopped farming. She eventually moved to the United States, where she began work as a farm laborer. After she had been in the United States for a few years, she started gardening on the rented land where she lives in northwestern Washington.

"One time we grew a lot of watermelon, and my husband asked what we were going to do with so much watermelon, so we started selling it." Victoria and her husband began planting crops in larger volume, and thirteen years ago, officially opened their farm business with their son and her brother. They now sell a diverse array of produce at Seattle-area farmers markets. Victoria talked about her struggle to send money to her family in Mexico. After working on another farm during the day, she comes home to work more hours on her own land. She is making just enough to keep her farm afloat and send money to her parents. "Well, my experience in Mexico was good, but it was also hard because my parents' economy was very poor. So I think being in this country gives me means and I can live a little better. And I can also give a little to my family and help them."

While living in the United States and struggling to make their own farms succeed, some farmers have established new farms in Mexico as well. This is the goal for Mario, who was eight years old when he started farming with his grandfather in his hometown in Oaxaca. Mario came to the United States when he was twelve years old with his sister and grandfather. Soon

Figure 4.2
Truck displaying a Mexican flag on a Latino/a farmers' field in California.

after immigrating, he began working on and off in the strawberry fields, dividing his time between farming and school. He wanted to make the transition to having his own farm at a young age, which according to him, was an additional challenge. "It was really hard for me because I was so young, and people wouldn't take me seriously and it was challenging." Mario now farms mostly strawberries with some mixed vegetables on California's Central Coast. He said, "My plan right now is to expand right here and then put a new business in Mexico." Most farmers who have succeeded in starting farms in their home country have family members maintaining the land for them, while others have helped family members buy or sustain landownership in Mexico themselves. Farmers like Mario see the United States as one home, and Mexico as another. Although they may not be able to cross the border easily themselves, the knowledge and culture they have brought are continually crossing back and forth, and they establish new agrarian spaces on both sides of the border.

Irrespective of their desire to stay in the United States or return to their home country, all the farmers I interviewed expressed a longing to re-create a sense of home in the United States for their immediate future. For them, as noted earlier, home was intimately connected to their agrarian culture and practices. Immigrant farmers' circumstances are complex, as they are oftentimes leaving one condition of rural poverty just to enter another. Yet the experience of growing food for ones' family in a space that one has relative power over is a dream that they aspire to as they adjust to a new ecology, economy, and culture. Their past informs their present, as they struggle to join local and business communities in a competitive and unforgiving field. As I discuss below, the draw to stay in agriculture is influenced by their experiences as former farmers and immigrants, which is evidenced by their particular farming approach.

Alternative Growing, or "Doing It the Old Way"

Many of the farmers involved in this study are coming from backgrounds of subsistence farming, where they grew diverse crop mixes, used minimal off-farm inputs, and often saved seeds each year. Now in the United States, they are producing a combination of fruits and vegetables, covering the spectrum of food demanded by farmers market customers as well as those that their own families and communities cannot easily find in the store. This includes Latin American specialty herbs like *mora* and *chepilin*, and vegetables such as *pipián* (a squash variety), tomatillos, and hot chiles, which are hard to find in many parts of the United States. They produce these for their own consumption as well as for Mexican and other immigrant customers. They also produce varieties preferred by US food aficionados, such as heirloom tomatoes and little gem lettuces, and crops requested by other immigrant communities such as Chinese long beans and eggplant varieties. In addition to growing small-scale and diverse crops, most are committed to growing using low amounts of synthetic inputs, frequently employing integrated pest management techniques. As I discuss in the following sections, choosing to grow with lower or no synthetic inputs is not only reflective of practices learned in Mexico but also related to a desire to make their farms safer and more accessible to their children and other family members.

Many farmers referenced their farming practices as "organic." As touched on earlier, in order to sell agricultural products using an organic label, a farm must be certified by the USDA, and follow regulations and standards set by the National Organic Program. These standards include growing produce only in soil where no prohibited substances (most synthetic pesticides and fertilizers) have been used for three years preceding harvest. In this book, I have specified if the farmer being quoted or discussed is a certified organic farmer whenever possible. For some farmers, the term "organic" is more conceptual, related to what they see as a more "natural" way of farming. For them, although they may or may not be certified organic for a variety of reasons, including the process and cost of certification (for more discussion of organic, see chapter 3), organic is a broader idea, reflecting farming practices that they learned in Mexico.

Their experiences of growing using low off-farm inputs and diverse cropping systems before emigrating provides many immigrant farmers with the knowledge to start as low-input farmers by default. David, mentioned in chapter 3, is a certified organic farmer in California. In his hometown in Michoacán, he told me, his family has a long tradition of growing food without synthetic additives, yet he only learned the term "organic" when he immigrated and began working on other peoples' farms. He worked for fifteen years picking berries for a large conventional berry producer before starting his own farm. He explained that he was hospitalized after being forced back into the fields immediately following a pesticide application while working in the berry fields. It was then that he decided it was time to look for a way to grow without pesticides and other synthetic inputs. He first learned about "organic" as a technical concept when he started as a student in the ALBA farmer training course in Salinas. "ALBA was doing a training to learn how to be your own boss and organic farmer. I didn't know what organic was until I went there and I asked, 'What's organic. What does organic mean?' ... As I learned what it was," says David, "I was like, oh, let's do it the old way." For him, the choice to return to farming without synthetic inputs was related to farming the "old way," as his family had in Mexico. His family grows beans and corn in addition to raising goats, cows, and horses, all for subsistence. While he is selling for the market, he notes that many of the crops he grows are inspired by those his father cultivated and were primarily consumed by his family at home. For example, he grows garbanzo beans and oats, which he combines with corn for tortillas, like his mother made when he was a child. It was during the ALBA training that he recognized his roots are in organic practices. "It's funny, I am telling people all the time that my parents and my brothers, I have six brothers in Mexico, they are organic too, but they don't know that. They are organic because they don't have resources to buy fertilizers and all that. So they are organic too." He points out that his family grows organically because that is their only choice economically. They do not have the money to buy synthetic additives, yet they do have available family labor to do the extra work. Rather than a decision related to a farming or ecological philosophy, it is simply what they can afford to do, given the resources they have.

On the other hand, Carlos in New York, quoted in the beginning of this chapter, farms using organic techniques in part because of the ways he saw his family's farm suffer in Mexico once they started using synthetic inputs. "We were organic, we just didn't know we were organic," he explains. "So that's what we want to go back to. ... It's ironic that people like my father or my uncles, when they got introduced to the chemicals and the commercial fertilizers, they were like, 'Oh, this is great.' And then it turns out they realized a decade later that you have to put it back into the soil every year or you get nothing." As I discuss in the next chapter, Carlos blames his family's uptake of synthetic additives on their need to compete with US imports of corn and wheat. This pressure to compete in the global agricultural market is, quite ironically, the underlying reason many immigrants leave farming and come to the United States to work in the first place.

Figure 4.3
Jacinto Sanchez of Sanchez Farm in Washington State.

Lucia came to the United States in the 1970s from Guerrero, where she grew up on her family's farm. After Lucia's mother was injured and disabled from a farmwork-related accident following immigration, Lucia and her family began the process of starting their own farming business. She is now a well-established farmer in California. Lucia told me, "We are traditional farmers. My grandparents were farmers in Mexico. ... So they were traditional farmers. This is what it is to us. Only here the system changes the name and the regulations, and there is a process to be a certified organic farmer."

Miguel, who is originally from Oaxaca, made similar comments, stating that his organic knowledge was rooted in the ways he farmed growing up. He is an evangelical Christian and told me he had to leave his hometown due to regional religious conflicts. He came to the United States twenty-five years ago to work in the fields and started his farm about ten years later. Miguel now grows certified organic berries and some vegetables on twenty-eight acres located in the Skagit Valley in Washington, selling mostly at farmers markets. He has a large family, and all his children are involved in his business. His adult son, who is fluent in English, manages the markets. When I visited his land, I met no less than four of his adult children harvesting in the fields. Miguel explained his reasoning for growing organically: "It's clean, it does not have any chemicals ... that's kosher. That's what we eat in Oaxaca, me and my father and everybody who lives in the mountain." He explicitly connects his farming practices to the foodways of his upbringing in Mexico. In this way, farming using particular organic practices allows him to extend that knowledge to life in a new place, where his own children are learning to farm using some of those same traditions.

Similarly, Victoria, a certified organic farmer introduced above, relates her organic practices to her desire to make her farm a space for cultural education. She wants her farm to be a place where her children can learn about their agricultural "roots" in organic practices. "I want my children to know how important it is to grow organicly and with no chemicals. I also want to show them their roots, how I taught myself these things since I was little."

Further, as I have noted above, most farmers have had some level of negative experiences working with pesticides and fumigants in their previous jobs. They are aware of the risk of the related illnesses, some having had firsthand experience, and do not wish to expose their families. This was mentioned in many of my interviews, and in several instances was the reason they decided to leave their employer and start their own farm. Gabriel is originally from Sinaloa, Mexico. Although he never owned land in his home country, he has extensive experience working in industrial garlic, lettuce, and strawberry production in both Mexico and the United States. Gabriel spoke about his previous work experience in conventional agriculture, observing, "Many pesticides—when we were in the fields the airplanes would fly over us and they would expel, I don't know how to say it. ... But during this time, we weren't told they were dangerous for us." He continued to describe the ways that this experience directly influenced his decision to grow organically. After fearing for his own health and that of his colleagues, he knew he needed to grow crops using methods that felt healthier and safer for him. As a small-scale farmer who plans to continue to practice agriculture with his own family, he could not apply the same kinds of additives that his former employers had exposed him to.

Aside from organic practices, immigrating with agricultural experience, of course, means immigrating with more general agricultural knowledge. Amado, came to the United States twenty-five years ago from Puebla. He noted that his knowledge of farming in the dry California landscape came from his experience growing in Mexico, saying, "The main thing is the plant should have no weeds, because if they have them, then they need more water." He brings this expertise to his own farm on the Central Coast— expertise he was unable to apply in his work as a farm laborer, where each task was assigned, and his input was never solicited. Comparatively, on his own farm, he can use this experience to re-create a farm that looks and feels like home.

These farmers, however, are not limiting themselves to growing practices learned prior to their immigration. Most farmers mix their experiences from various points in the lives, as farmers and workers, in both Mexico and the United States. Additionally, farmers have had to learn new techniques to adjust to different climates and markets in the United States. Technologies like drip irrigation and tractors are welcomed advances for many, creating less demand on their physical labor and allowing them to produce the quantities needed to compete in US markets.

Many farmers have learned to grow crops that they had never cultivated before, exhibiting the ability to adjust and adapt to demands when necessary. Andres is a certified organic farmer in California. He identifies as indigenous, from the Mixteco region of Oaxaca. He and his wife had been renting land and farming in the United States for two years when I met them. His wife had to leave her farmworker position after she was injured on the job. When her employer refused to pay her disability, they decided it was time to start their own farm, and Andres enrolled in the ALBA farmer training in the Salinas Valley. They focus on selling heirloom tomatoes directly to grocery stores, although they grow other crops on the side for their family's consumption. "For ten years, I worked in the fields [as an employee]. In Oaxaca, I was also working on the fields. So all my life I've been working in the fields. Here, I learned how to sow, the distances, water quantities, hours, when you plant, and when you harvest. ... In Oaxaca [we farmed] only for eating. We only planted corn, beans, and zucchini. But once I arrived here, I learned how to grow other vegetables, beets, lettuce, and stuff." Andres notes that he gained agricultural knowledge on both sides of the border. He uses both experiences, as a worker and farmer, to inform his cultivation practices in the United States. He continued, commenting, "Everything that I've ever done, I've done it in the fields. I know how to work the land, how to plant, how to water, use seeds. I know almost everything."

In addition to replicating a familiar farming technique, low inputs combined with higher levels of crop diversity also means the farmer has the ability to provide an organically grown (or at least, less contaminated) and diverse diet for his or her family. The importance of family was brought up in almost all my interviews, in all regions of the country. Farmers, male and female, consistently reinforced the relationship between their decision to farm in a particular way and their ability to create the life they wanted for their children, extended family, and larger community, as part of re-creating a home. In the next two sections, I discuss the continuation of family culture and sharing of knowledge as well as the value placed on farming as a part of a healthy family model and way of life.

Feeding and Teaching Family and Community

This alternative style of growing reflects not only an economic choice but also one grounded in a way of life, as it allows farmers to prioritize their family's consumption and health, oftentimes over capital. Even the most economically successful farmers I interviewed said making sure their family is well fed by their crops is their primary motivation for farming, while selling in the market came second. These practices come from a tradition of connecting food production with familial and community priorities. For the farmers I spoke with, it was not enough to purchase healthy food for their family; growing this food connects them to the cultural practices that are familiar to them and that they associate with a sense of home.

"Peppers, corn, pumpkin, zucchini, yellow squash, little gems, heirloom tomatoes, berries, cilantro, a little *pápalo* over here." A farmer in California lists all the crops he is growing as we walk through his field. This happened in almost every one of my farmer interviews; at some point as we walked, they started to list the wide variety of crops they were growing, usually without prompting. In all the regions I visited, one of the most striking differences between Latino/a immigrant and white farmers was their crop diversity. White farmers, by contrast, were more likely to grow a monocrop or two-to-three-crop rotation. Growing fewer crops allows for a more controlled spatial configuration, including more uniform rows and consistency throughout their fields, as compared to their immigrant counterparts.[4] For immigrant farmers, growing a diversity of crops is part of sustaining themselves both practically and culturally.

Lucia, introduced above, explains that she makes a concerted effort to incorporate a variety of crops into their fields, including some from their previous diets in Mexico. "It's a mix [between Mexico and the United States]. It's a mix because we try to include a plan to plant Mexican products." This way, she can feed her family and community familiar foods as well as continue culinary traditions through her farm.

Prioritizing the provision of healthy and diverse diets for their families and communities, including particular foods often missing from their lives after migration, stems from their background as subsistence farmers and puts them somewhat at odds with the push to grow in the most economically competitive form possible (see Minkoff-Zern 2014a, 2014b). Even when their crop diversity has been reduced due to market pressures, most families still grow a small plot of traditional milpa crops—a combination of corn, squash, and beans—alongside a field of tomatoes or strawberries. Lucia explains her reasoning for prioritizing the cultivation of foods her family can eat versus food only for the market: "In reality, if we are to conserve our health, our bodies, and our children's bodies, so they don't have obesity when they are young, is to return to cooking. Return again to our diet, to eat greens, squash, corn, seasonal fruits. I feel that it is time for change, time to do this."

Beyond just consumption, these practices are tied to cultural food traditions, rooted in growing, not simply consuming, food. As Carlos told me, "We have an eight-year-old ... and we explain to him why he has to eat vegetables, and why they have to be local, and why they have to be organic." Their farm in the Finger Lakes region is a place where he and his wife feel they can model an agrarian way of life for their son. It is not enough to purchase this food; they want him to see where it is grown, and that this is something he can learn to do as well. They want to pass on to him their

Figure 4.4
Corn planted alongside kale at a Latino/a farm in California.

tradition of consuming food that is grown in their community, and held to a high standard for environmental and human safety.

Mario, who spoke above of starting a farm in Mexico, also talked about the importance of feeding people, in addition to his need to make a profit. He notes that his affinity for feeding people is rooted in his experience growing up in a farming family, saying, "Because, it was like a dream for me. When I was little and I was farming, I liked to farm and I liked to grow plants, and I liked to help people and feed people. It's not only because I want to make money; to me, it is also because I feel good seeing people eating this." While he does not disregard the fact that he needs to make a living, he emphasizes the significance of feeding people. Of course he is not only referring to his family but also the larger community of people that eat the food he grows.

Like Mario, Maria stresses the importance of feeding her broader community as a priority for her in farming. Maria is fifty years old and belongs to a farming cooperative in Minnesota. Although she does not have a

Figure 4.5
Dried peppers sold by a Latino/a farmer at a farmers market in California.

background as a farmworker herself, she worked as an advocate for farmworker health before starting her farm. She was direct in describing the relationship between her choice to farm and the continued chemical exposure her family and community experienced as workers in the fields. Her connection to farming and organic food began at a young age. She talks about the food she ate growing up in Mexico, commenting, "I was raised on organic food without knowing that it was organic." She states that her family and extended community couldn't afford organic produce in the United States, but they know the difference; they know that is what they want to eat. Her farm sells to a marketing cooperative, which outreaches to larger Twin Cities outlets, but she also conducts direct sales in her immediate community through word of mouth and sometimes by going door-to-door in apartment buildings with large immigrant farmworker populations. Her experience helps her connect the health of farmworkers to that of consumers, as she reflects on her role as both a producer and eater of food. "The more you buy conventional food, the more you support the mistreatment of farmworkers—pesticides are very dangerous. Not just for the workers, but for us who eat the food."

Andres also related his previous work in conventional fields to his own health and his choice to grow organically on his farm. "The ones who use fertilizer ... all of it goes to our bodies. And you also contaminate the land; we are hurting the land." He followed this remark by identifying a connection between poisoning his body and contaminating the land. For those who have physically labored in agriculture, their own body and the ecosystem they live in are inseparable.

For some farmers, planting diverse crops is not only reminiscent of their lives in Mexico but also expands their diets. Jorge farms with his wife, Estela, and his in-laws in Minnesota. According to him, the ones with agricultural experience are Estela and her parents. It was her idea to start their own business. "She saw a flyer [for a farmer training program] and told me about it. I didn't pay attention at first, but then I told her that we could do it if she wanted to and that I'll support her." Jorge adds, "We can also eat healthy. I've eaten things that I've never eaten before." He points out that the food they grow is not just healthier for consumers but for themselves as farmworkers and farm owners too.

Many of the farmers I interviewed related a particular style of land-based living with good health and longevity. They frequently associated healthy living with small-scale farming and gardening, as their parents and grandparents had practiced in Mexico. Silvio, a farmer in Minnesota, explains, "In our story from Mexico, our grandparents lived long because they harvest their own stuff. In Guadalajara, there is no agriculture like here [in the United States], only small gardens. My grandparents planted and harvested one or two things, and they lived a long time."

For these farmers, incorporating their partners, parents, and older children on the farm is also directly related to their choice to use limited synthetic inputs. Their interest in protecting their families from toxic farm additives as well as providing a safe place to spend time together and take part in long-held generational practices leads them to a more alternative form of growing. Saul, introduced earlier in this chapter, explains, "You can arrive to a field and eat something right there without worrying about having chemicals or some disease. ... I compare an organic garden with a backyard; [it] is almost like a family environment."

Providing their families and communities with food that they produce is part of what drives immigrant farmers to stay in agriculture. It is directly connected to their choice to grow diverse crops versus monocrops, and use low or no synthetic inputs, as they are intimately familiar with the toxicity of industrial farming practices and want to provide an alternative for their family. Further, this kind of food, which many of them identify as organic, is reminiscent of a diet and way of producing from their own past. It is through extending those practices that their farm becomes a place to continue and root their agricultural and culinary identity. In the next section, I build on this idea of family cross-border connections through food, exploring the role of the family on the physical farm.

Family Labor and Knowledge

On many farms I visited, I saw toddlers playing and napping nearby the fields, teenagers helping pick and sell produce at markets on the weekends, and elderly parents packing produce. Most of the farm owners I interviewed are couples who employ their teenage or adult children, and sometimes other extended family such as cousins and grandparents. All farmers, with the exception of a few, employ some family labor. Most work side by side with relatives on a daily basis. Oftentimes, more family members come to help during a particularly busy part of the harvest season. Many told me they would like to keep it that way; they did not want to take on the task of finding outside labor or manage the complications of hiring strangers. I discuss the complexities of labor, including hired labor, in more depth in chapter 5. Here I focus on how family labor reinforces familial agrarian knowledge, tradition, and culture.

Sara is originally from Jalisco, where her father taught her to farm. "He always brought us to the field. We grew corns, beans, and pumpkin." After many years working for other farmers, Sara and her husband, Ernesto, decided to look for opportunities to begin their own farm. For the past four years, they have owned and operated a mixed-vegetable farm in the Skagit Valley of Washington. I asked Sara why she started a farm instead of another kind of business, especially when it is such a challenging business to get into. Her answer revolved around her family:

So we can teach our kids to like farming. Yesterday we came to plant the corn with our two children, and both were doing something, so we want to teach them that so they can see the plants growing and harvested. You can't do that in other types of work; you can't bring your kids. That's why having your own business is good. ... There are other type of businesses, but we started with this because we both come from the country. We both like it, and we want our kids to like it too. When they grow up, they can decide if they want to do it or not.

Alejandro echoed this sentiment. "I teach them, not for them to start working, but so they can learn and value all this." He made it clear that for his children to learn about farming and food-related practices was more than teaching them a skill; it was teaching them to value his family's agrarian culture and traditions.

Although almost all the farms I visited were owned and operated by separate and distinct nuclear families, resources and knowledge were commonly shared among extended immigrant families. Many of them have been in the United States for over twenty years, yet most of the immigrant generation still speaks primarily Spanish, with just enough English-language ability to navigate markets. They depend on their teenage and adult children to communicate with market managers, equipment salespeople, government representatives, and other neighbors. In many cases, their children manage promotion and selling at markets. As Alejandro explains, "We know very little English. Sometimes the kids help us, but sometimes the kids don't want to [laughs]. It's a little embarrassing." This language barrier, while it keeps immigrant communities somewhat isolated among largely white and English-speaking broader regional populations, functions to maintain closeness among immigrant farming families because they depend on each other before looking to outsiders for assistance.

After watching their parents struggle to transition from farmworkers to small business owners, many of the adult-aged children of farm owners said that they wanted to help their parents' businesses grow. Marco, who owns and operates a farm with his parents in Virginia, emigrated from Jalisco about twenty years ago. He noted that his area is unique in having so many farmers of Mexican origin. This makes them feel comfortable and has given them a reason to stay. He explained that for his parents, who both migrated throughout the United States as farmworkers before settling in Virginia, having their own farm in the United States was always their dream. "My parents always talked about having acres. Having a country home. Having pigs, cows, and chickens, and growing your stuff, and whatever goes bad, give it to them to fatten up." He also told me that farming and living in rural Virginia feels like home. "This is what I know. I go to the cities and come in through the bridge, ... and I'm just like, 'Oh, I'm home.' I guess it's just the country life. It's very peaceful. I don't know what it is." Establishing a stable agrarian life in the Northern Neck allowed his parents to realize the lifestyle they wanted for themselves and their children after many years traveling from place to place.

Farmers repeatedly commented that they didn't want their farms to become too large; they preferred to maintain the scale of a homestead. Oftentimes those with farms between ten and forty acres expressed no desire to grow in size. They were working as hard as they could to make ends meet and did not see scaling up as a goal. Additionally, they were struggling to sell the produce they already grew. Instead of aspiring to cultivate more acres, they were focused on finding stronger markets for their current products. Camilia, a California farmer who was selling wholesale and trying to enter farmers markets, told me, "We don't want to start with a big ranch. It is better little by little." Carlos echoed that sentiment, saying, "Our ideal goal would be to farm a small acreage where we can make a living and do what we like for a living." The desire to maintain a small-scale farm, despite pressures to grow in size, was an ongoing theme throughout my interviews, as farmers saw their farms as their homes and not simply businesses with a goal of expansion.

Moreover, for some farmers it is a way to provide more career options for their children. Although some of their children have worked as farm laborers to make extra cash, most have grown up on family owned farms and have been educated in the United States. Not all farmers want their children to take over their farm operation, yet many see farming as a good profession for their children, if they are interested. Although farming is not the easiest professional choice, it is an experience they are able to offer in terms of technical skills and knowledge, and one that reinforces their family's agrarian culture and heritage.

Pablo felt strongly that if he started his own farm, it would be a positive influence on his children's lives, and create a healthy space and example for them to live by. "I saw that there was money [to start my own farm], and so I brought my kids with me. I said, 'No more working for other people.' I took my kids so they wouldn't be on the streets. ... What really made me do this was my kids; they were going down the wrong path." Diego, a farmer introduced in chapter 3, made a similar comment that while he doesn't expect his children will all become farmers like him, it will demonstrate a work ethic to help them survive economically and culturally. "It's more like trying to teach them and trying to give them good habits." Most farmers emphasized that they want their children to get a formal education as well. Rodrigo grew up in Michoacán, working with his parents in their family's fields. After immigrating to the United States, he gained many years of industrial agricultural experience, mostly working in strawberry production. In 2012, he started a farming cooperative in Minnesota with some partners, including Maria, mentioned above. Regarding his children, Rodrigo told me, "After they finish their studies, they can decide if they are interested in agriculture or not." Many also noted that the farm can help their children pay for college, if they choose, and they can bring that education back to help with the family business or to use it toward accomplishing their own, nonagrarian goals.

One farmer's son told me that although his father encourages him to think broadly about his future, he sees farming as a skill he will always have, should he need it. "My dad tells me, one day, if you don't have a job and you want to do something, you already know how to farm." Having learned how to farm, their children have a lifelong skill they can use—the same skill they were taught by their own parents before immigration. Passing on this knowledge and ability is part of a tradition, and while it is not an obligation, they can provide a legacy that their children can fall back on when needed.

Antonia, a farmer in Virginia, told me that although she did not expect all her children to farm, she wanted them to be proud of their agricultural background and know that they always have farming skills as a backup plan to make a living. "I tell my kids, 'You don't want to do it [farming]. Stay in school. Stay in school, but just don't forget where you came from. There's always, you always will find a job farming, in case you don't find whatever you want to do. You can always come back. There's nobody who's going to tell you, "Oh, you don't know how to do it." Yes you do. Yes you do.'" She made it clear that their farming tradition is something she wants them to be proud of and see as part of an identity that connects them to their family's history and survival.

Alejandro, who spoke above of farming by hand in Mexico, explains that he not only wants his children to learn farming skills and the agrarian practices of their family but also wants his children to understand and value his own work experience and traditions, as a legacy of struggle and persistence. "I teach them, not for them to start working, but so they can learn and value all this. Someday we will retire and we will leave all this to them, and then they will know how much we struggle to have this," Alejandro says. "Unfortunately, I have seen children who lose their father and they don't value what their father did; they don't appreciate it because they don't really know the efforts that it took."

Regardless of whether or not their children choose to farm, incorporating their family on the farm is also a way for immigrant farmers to ensure that their children are exposed to agrarian expertise and ethos, and a way of life somewhat similar to what they remember from growing up in rural Mexico. In the next section, I look at nondiversified farmers, who defy many of the observations and arguments I have presented in this book. Although their farms may look different than those discussed above, I found they still emphasize some of the same goals and reasons for farming as growers who use more alternative practices, particularly when it comes to re-creating a sense of home.

Nondiversified Immigrant Farmers

Although the majority of farmers I interviewed across the country fit the description of an alternative farmer, I also met some who were an exception to the trends I was seeing. Nondiversified farmers focus on primarily one crop or type of crop, and in the cases discussed below, grow using conventional or nonorganic practices (with the exception of one organic apple farmer). More often, compared to the majority direct sales of alternative growers I interviewed, they sell to wholesale purchasers or packinghouses. I met immigrant farmers in both Washington and California who met this portrait. The stories of nondiversified immigrant farmers, which in my research ranged from tree fruit farmers to strawberry growers (although I am sure there are immigrant farmers in other monocrops as well), follow many of the same trajectories of alternative or more diversified farmers. They came from farming communities in Mexico, worked as farm laborers before starting their own businesses, and spoke of a desire to maintain a connection to the land for themselves and their families. I would argue that the difference in these regions is the endurance of the Mexican immigrant community, which has allowed for a second generation to establish itself in supportive roles for newer immigrants, such as at the USDA, combined with a strong need for a new cohort of farmers to step in where growers' children are not interested. While their practices look different, I found many commonalities, especially their stress on re-creating an agrarian culture and livelihood, and the incorporation of their families on the farm.

Tree Fruit Orchards

My introduction to a community of Mexican immigrant tree orchardists was during one of my research trips to Washington. I drove from Skagit County, on the west coast of the state, and an area where I had met many immigrant mixed-vegetable farmers, to the FSA office in Wenatchee. Wenatchee, in the central part of Washington, is the heart of tree fruit country, and sometimes referred to as "Appleland" or the "Apple Capital of the World." In Wenatchee and the surrounding area of Chelan County, conventional apples, cherries, pears, and peaches are produced for global shipping.

The farms in the area are not agriculturally diverse; diverse in this region means multiple varieties of apples or cherries. Most orchards are conventional, and all growers sell their crop to industrial-scale packinghouses. Farmers do not need to personally promote their products, unlike those in direct markets. The packinghouses pursue the farmers, seeking to buy their fruit. Growers are only responsible to grow the fruit and transport it to the packer, who sorts, washes, grades, and packs it. The orchards are capital intensive, from the land to the machinery to the investment in the plants, which take years to mature for harvest.

These farmers are the same general demographic as the immigrant alternative farmers I interviewed. All were first-generation immigrants who started as farmworkers in the United States. Most had little formal education, and while some had better English-speaking abilities than other farmers I met, most did not. The packinghouses are also managed by Latino/as, making it possible for immigrant farmers to sell their product without speaking English. One large difference with these farmers is that in order to purchase the land and business, they had to be in the United States legally, as all of them went through the FSA for a farm loan. Without a loan, the investment needed would be prohibitive to a farmworker.

Without taking a deeper look, it doesn't seem likely that any immigrant workers could possibly move their way up the ladder in this region. The land and farming operations are expensive to purchase, requiring massive capital inputs as well an ability to standardize production—all the barriers that cause most immigrant farmers to grow using more alternative and less capital-intensive methods. From what I learned through Washington State University extension and the USDA offices there, however, there are quite a few who have made this transition.

On arriving in Wenatchee, I drove directly to the FSA office, where I met with José Limon, one of the FSA officers in the region and also the son of an immigrant farmer. José first introduced me to his father, Jesus, quoted in chapter 3, who was in the office waiting for me when I arrived.

Jesus is in his mid-sixties and, in the 1980s, was one of the first immigrant orchardists in the state. He is also the only immigrant fruit tree grower I interviewed who was certified organic. He told me that when he started his farm, there were only two or three other Latino/a farmers in the region. He came from Mexico to work in the orchards, with barely a grade school education and no ability to speak English. He now owns hundreds of acres of apples and has dozens of people who work on his crews. Like other immigrant orchardists I met in the area, he sells to packinghouses, grows only tree fruit, and is commercially oriented in his approach to farming. He was incredibly proud to quote his sales and profits in specific terms. When I asked Jesus what motivated him to start farming, he said it was both the familiar agricultural way of life and desire for autonomy. "I grew up on farms. I think part of it is lifestyle and part of it is wanting to be your own boss. Probably fifty-fifty. It's a lot harder to do it because you have to make economic decisions, and how to open the road in front was the hardest part." In our interview, he made it clear that one of the key differences he sees between himself and white orchard owners is that he still loves working in the fields, and does so on a regular basis. As I describe in chapter 5, he is oftentimes mistaken by new employees for being a worker himself. Workers are accustomed to seeing their bosses as physically separate from the crew, both in their physical activities and their racial as well as ethnic presentation, and Jesus's presence in the fields, especially on such a large operation, was an anomaly for them.

Later in the day, his son, José, took me on a tour through the region, introducing me to several farmers who are part of a small community of orchardists who were also first-generation immigrants from Mexico. Like other farmers I interviewed, many spoke of the importance of family, and teaching their children about agrarian livelihoods and work ethic by having them work in the fields beside them. They asserted that they relied heavily on their family's labor as an asset to start their business. Although many also hired nonfamily labor, they all spoke about the fact that they work alongside their crews.

All the orchardists I met, with the exception of one, bought the farm directly from their former employer. Usually they were the field manager for many years first. Many orchardists are close to retirement age and have no children who want to take over the farm—a trend among farmers across the country (USDA 2014). As they retire from farming, they have to make a choice: sell to a big land investor who may or may not keep it in farming, sell to another white farmer who wants to expand their operation, or sell to one of their workers, who has the knowledge and has put in sweat equity, and will keep it producing using the same methods and on a similar scale. According to Limon, he thinks about 5 to 10 percent of retiring farmers are choosing this option, based on who he observes coming in for farm loans. The loans are necessary to get started on their own farms, as the capital investment is high. The farmers doing this are selling below market value, and selling not only their land but also their business, including their contracts with the packinghouses, their machinery, and their established relationships with workers. They are doing it because they want to pass it on to another small-scale farmer and have had a good relationship with a manager, not because it is the most financially advantageous thing to do.

Also, unlike most farmers I interviewed, orchardists said they would like to grow larger if they could. With the exception of Jesus, who has some organic acreage in addition to conventional, most seemed content continuing to grow using the same techniques and approaches that their bosses did, and did not have much interest in organic, becoming more diverse, or accessing direct markets. That said, they spoke of home gardens and feeding their families from what they grew when possible.

Some farmers told me they had almost no money to start, so their boss helped them out on top of getting an FSA loan. While this is incredibly generous, José highlighted the fact that when they buy the farm, the previous owner usually keeps the house on the property, if there is one. This prevents the new farmer from living on-site, and sustains the paternal relationship between their previous boss and the immigrant farmer. While orchardists certainly fulfill many of the same agricultural goals as other immigrant farmers, especially in terms of escaping their class position as workers, living off the farm site limits them in achieving their full agrarian vision.

Strawberries

Orchardists in Washington are by no means the only first-generation Mexican farmers who do not fit the alternative farmer model. As the census shows, at least regarding those who identify as Hispanic/Latino, there are thousands of Latino/a farmers managing large- to small-scale agricultural operations, including raising cattle and other livestock, and cultivating grains, nuts, fruits, and vegetables in all forms.[5]

The California Strawberry Commission, in particular, has been purposefully highlighting Hispanic/Latino farmers for the past several years. In its 2014 report, *Growing the American Dream: California Strawberry Farming's Rich History of Immigrants and Opportunity*, and on the commission's website in a section titled "American Dream," it estimates that 65 percent of all the state's strawberry farmers are of Mexican American descent. The commission also claims that about 25 percent of these Latino/a strawberry farmers started out as field workers and worked their way up to become farm owners.

In addition to the report, in 2015 the commission elected Latina strawberry grower Lorena Chavez as board chair. She is the first Latino/a to be elected to this position. Her father came to California as a Bracero farmworker. In a 2015 article in the *Packer*, a publication for the packing industry, the commission president, Rick Tomlinson, is quoted from a news release as saying, "Lorena Chavez embodies everything positive that strawberries represent to California. Her family's personal story is a prime example of how immigrants have found opportunity and a path to achieving the American dream through hard work in California's strawberry fields" (Hornick 2015).

In a phone conversation I had with Carolyn O'Donnell, the communications director at the commission, she commented on why she thinks strawberries are a good fit for immigrants as they look to enter farming. She pointed out that strawberries do not require heavy machinery or the related capital inputs. Strawberries are fragile and thus still have not been totally mechanized. Rather, the crop requires a lot of labor, and immigrants have an advantage because of their extended family networks. "They can get a lot of fruit off a small plot of land. They don't need to have trees, [or] bushes, [and] not a lot of machinery. Strawberries are hand planted, harvested, [and] weeded, and that doesn't require a lot of investment."

What she said certainly corroborates with what I found in my research concerning opportunities for immigrant growers. It is true that smaller-scale growers may benefit greatly from access to family labor. And crops, like strawberries, that require less machinery and can be profitable on a small plot of land are an easier entry point to the market as compared to crops such as wheat or corn.

Yet despite this story depicting opportunities for Latino/as to get ahead in the industry, when I asked O'Donnell about openings for recent immigrants, she confirmed my own findings that industrial farming is not welcoming, especially for those who are undocumented. She told me, "The latest wave of newer [strawberry] famers are those who were able to become legal before amnesty reform in the eighties. I can't say how many have arrived in the past twenty years. ... My impression is that they need to be legal. Everyone has documentation, but there is a difference between someone who is legal and someone who has documentation."[6] As she reiterates with this statement, not having legal status in the US means farmers are potentially going to face more challenges to their growth and stability as business owners.

She told me that the commission put out the report to reflect the demographic changes in the industry over the past several decades rather than to intentionally change its reputation or image. The Latino/a farmers whom the commission highlights, however, are not reflective of those who are currently working in the fields, and have little opportunity to move up the labor chain from worker to owner, especially given industrial agriculture standards. Since the vast majority of field workers are undocumented, this leaves the majority out of the opportunity to enter the industry as a grower.[7]

While I do not doubt that there are many first-generation immigrant farmers in the United States who do not fit the description of alternative farmers I have given in this book, claims that anyone can move up the agricultural ladder from farmworker to farm owner are, under most contexts, incorrect. As I have tried to make clear throughout the book, it is due to immigrant farmers' limitations as well as their specific knowledge and skill set that first-generation immigrant farmers are following a particular alternative approach rather than getting into the kind of industrial mode of production in which they labor as farmworkers. Yet as I have described here, immigrant farmers are defying the odds in a vast number of ways in order to achieve their agrarian dream.

Crossing Borders, Overcoming Boundaries

As Javier, one of the few farmers who grows cooperatively with other immigrant farmers on a collective farm in Minnesota, told me, "We bring our experience from Mexico, from when we were young. ... The cooperative is called Agua Gorda because that was the farm that we come from. I think we named it like that as a thank you." The naming of their farm represents the memories that they bring with them of their agrarian life in Mexico as well as a sense of gratitude for the skills that their experience has provided them.

Despite struggling against deep-rooted racial and ethnic agrarian hierarchies, immigrant farmers are starting their own farms, where they reestablish agricultural livelihoods and foodways. They cultivate not only to sustain themselves financially but also as a way to re-create a new sense of place and home—one that has been complicated by many years of economic and cultural dislocation. After being dispossessed from their homelands by transnational agricultural policies and forced to work as migrant laborers in the global industrial food system, these farmers are in part motivated by a desire to reclaim a land-based identity, stripped from them via the processes of migration. Through the practice of then repossessing land and their own labor, they then recross the class border, again claiming the means of production as their own.

In my research, I found there are many first-generation immigrant farmers embracing what can be identified as alternative practices to the industrial agricultural mainstream. In part, this is due to their limitations in accessing land and resources. But they are also doing this purposefully, to feed their families and communities in a way they deem healthy. Yet other immigrant farmers are modeling a different kind of farming—one that is more reflective of US industrial agriculture. Both of these groups of farmers are growing food as a way to reconnect with their families' agricultural

Figure 4.6
Farmers at Agua Gorda cooperative farm in Minnesota working on assembling a plastic mulch layer on their farm.

traditions from their home countries and create opportunities for their children.

For many immigrant farmers, establishing a farm is not only a survival strategy but also a way to create a new life in the United States—one where they are able to build on their culture as food producers to create a space of their own. Their nostalgia for home draws on both an idea of the past and dream for the future. In establishing farms in the United States, workers cross geopolitical, class, and racial borders as they strive to re-create memories of what attachments to land and food mean to them. Looking forward to establishing a real home, they borrow from notions of an idealized one, ultimately creating a hybrid version of the place they remember combined with the realities of a new life.

5 Shifting the Means of Production: Food Sovereignty, Labor, and the Freedom to Farm

They took my house, my land. So I left, and I took my hands with me.
—Joaquín, an immigrant farmer from Oaxaca, now settled on California's Central Coast

When I decided to work for myself, I was working for someone else. I saw that after I worked for him for about five years, ... he was becoming successful, making a lot of money. And I stayed the same, earning $6 an hour. ... One day I said to him, "To start, this is good. But now I see that you're just there doing nothing, and I don't make anything. I don't make money. I'm the only one working." Because I was the only employee he had. ... He had at least $250,000 in earnings that I had made for him. And I said, "No, I'm killing myself for you. It's over. I'm going to start my own business." And that's how it happened.
—Martin

Martin, introduced in chapter 3, came to the United States when he was twenty-one from Guadalajara, and labored as a farmworker for twenty-seven years before saving enough money to start his own farm in the Northern Neck of Virginia. For him, the ability to work independently, make his own schedule, and see the products he cultivated benefit his own family made the transition to owning his own business a priority. He clearly depicts the dynamic between his former employer and himself: he provided the labor to produce the goods for market, and his boss received all the profits of his labor. Once he was able to, he shifted his position by starting his own farm, thereby reclaiming control over his own labor and the profit his work produced.

At the core of Martin's story is the process of agricultural laborers reclaiming the means of production—a process being promoted on a global scale by actors in the movement for food sovereignty. Food sovereignty, a transnational agrarian movement rooted in the idea that food is a human right, has been instituted internationally over the past several decades by the farmer coalition La Via Campesina. Its membership spans 81 countries and 182 organizations, including over 200,000,000 self-identified peasant farmer activists (La Via Campesina 2018). Farmers and advocates identifying with the food sovereignty movement aim to transform the global food system by addressing core inequalities in food distribution and resource access from the local to the global scale, unbalanced power in the food system, gender violence, and ecologically unsustainable practices (Patel 2009; Trauger 2017; Wittman, Desmarais, and Wiebe 2010). The farmers interviewed for this book, although they have not specifically articulated identifying with the movement themselves, reflect many of these ideals. In this chapter, I argue that as they strive for partial autonomy from a hierarchical and exploitative labor system, and in turn gain control over their own food production and consumption, they are enacting food sovereignty as a practice in their daily lives. But as I explain, it is a version of food sovereignty riddled with restraints and contradictions.

Starting their own farm businesses allows immigrant farmers the independence to make decisions on their farms regarding their growing practices, and perhaps more important, their own daily schedules and livelihood strategies. They start their farms with the primary goal of maintaining independence from their previous employers and agribusiness wages, and returning to their former livelihoods as farmers. As many farmers discussed with me, the "freedom" to farm was significant to them in both reestablishing a food-producing livelihood and reclaiming power over their own time. Rather than following the day-to-day instructions of others, these immigrant farmers now have increased control over farming practices and techniques as well as their own labor.

Central to their autonomy are the ways that immigrant farmworkers turned farmers challenge the classic Marxian capitalist trajectory, which predicts that dispossessed peasant farmers simply become industrial laborers. By avoiding hiring nonfamily workers, many farmers are evading recreating the same capitalist class formations that they labored under as hired farmworkers themselves.[1] By some definitions, these farmers are representative of petty or simple commodity production, in contrast to capitalist production, which is dependent on wage or paid laborers (Goodman and Redclift 1985). Yet these farmers certainly do not constitute a barrier to capitalist development, as previous discussions of the agrarian question would suggest (Kautsky 1988). In fact, immigrant producers in the United States provide a surprising and noteworthy example of how agriculture adapts to flows of capital, and how agricultural and capitalist relations take multiple and unexpected forms when observed closely (Henderson 1998; Wells 1984, 1996). Despite this fact, the transition from worker to owner demonstrates the potential for shifts in social relations and power dynamics in global food production, as workers are able to move beyond their race- and citizenship-based positions in the capitalist agrarian system.[2]

Both food sovereignty activists and agrarian studies scholars use the term "peasant" to identify farmers who are relatively autonomous from industrial agriculture. Farmers I met oftentimes used the Spanish term for the word "peasant," "campesino/a," to describe themselves both before and after migration. Jan Douwe van der Ploeg (2012, 2013, 2014) contends that peasant farmers are the necessary social force to further the movement for agroecological farming practices as well as the global movement for food sovereignty.[3] While I hesitate to directly identify the farmers in my study as peasant farmers per se, since they focus on commercial production and not subsistence, certainly their experiences fit the description of the ongoing struggle for autonomy from the industrial food system. As van der Ploeg (2012, 49) observes, "It might be argued that peasant farming is an ongoing struggle for autonomy—for the creation of a self-controlled resource base that allows for farming in a way that coincides with the interests, experiences and prospects of the peasant family."

The majority of farmers interviewed were explicitly averse to engaging with social movement politics, or identifying with any politically oriented or activist group, farming or otherwise, yet their rationale and motivation to start their own farms is undeniably in line with those of the global food sovereignty movement. In particular, the desire and goal for autonomy from their agricultural employers as well as independence from the system of industrial agricultural more broadly is reflective of the food sovereignty principles of agrarian reform as well as increased democratic control over the food system (Alonso-Fradejas et al. 2015; Wittman, Desmarais, and Wiebe 2010). As Amy Trauger (2017, 30) eloquently writes, "Food sovereignty is as much about changing systems of production as it is about something more fundamental and perhaps more ontologically threatening

Figure 5.1
Rufino Ventura, of Ventura Family Organic Farm, on his farm in California.

to capitalist modernity: the transformation of meaning, primarily around land, labor and exchange."

In theory, immigrant farmers represent this transformation of meaning, land, and labor. The trend and preference among immigrant farmers toward family labor instead of hired labor represents both a strong form of resistance to a purely capitalist labor structure and a key point of tension as some farms struggle to make ends meet economically. This resistance is representative of the larger movement of farmers and eaters who are pushing for a more democratically controlled and less exploitative food system, while contending with the constraints of current global food markets.

Yet as business owners, they are actively engaging with a capitalist system, and subject to market pressures to replicate the same industrial practices and workplace injustices that they once labored under. As many immigrant farmers have already scaled up and begun to hire nonfamily labor, they are stuck in the same labor and class hierarchies that they attempted to escape, only now they are on the other end of the relationship as employers. They are struggling to maintain these practices as they are pressured to grow their business in order to compete with other producers in their region, as well as globally, forcing some farmers to transition to a more industrial farming approach. As I demonstrate below, the potential for transforming the racial and ethnic makeup of agrarian labor relations is limited by current market constraints.

In this chapter, I address these contradictions as farmers grapple with maintaining family labor in the context of a highly competitive and global agricultural market. Using food sovereignty as a frame to understand their juxtaposition to the industrial food system, I look into the inherent contradictions in immigrant farmers' condition as both resisters and reproducers of a particular kind of capitalist agrarian structure, and the nuances of their role in the food system. I discuss the challenges inherent in shifting class positions, and what these mean for the broader labor politics of this transition. To fully appreciate the formation of their agrarian perspectives and class standing, I start with a brief history of agrarianism and land concentration, distribution, and reform in Mexico.

Land Reform, Dispossession, and the Rise and Fall of the *Ejido*

Owning a farm business engenders specific political and personal meaning for former peasant farmers and farmworkers, who have been deprived of the ability to survive off their land. Unlike most white farmers in the United States, Mexican immigrant farmers have been historically dispossessed from their land and resources through the ongoing processes of colonialism, international development, and globalization (McMichael 2013). Their position as racialized workers did not begin when they crossed the border into the United States; it has a much deeper history rooted in colonial dispossession and transnational agrifood policy. Despite this history, an important shift is occurring in agrarian class and race politics in the United States. Albeit at a small scale, immigrants are reclaiming control over their own labor, land, and the power to produce sustenance for themselves, their families, their community, and the larger consumer market. As I discuss in the following section, it is imperative to recognize the historic and geographic context of this change to fully appreciate its social importance.

From the time of European conquest through the relatively recent signing of NAFTA, outside forces have usurped land and labor from the native and peasant populations of Mexico, the ancestors of the immigrant farmers interviewed for this book. This historic and continued removal of native and peasant people from arable land has directly impacted the flow of immigrants across the border looking for work in the United States today.[4]

Colonial expansion and the process of the global dispossession of peasants from their land and resources began when Spanish conquistadores invaded the region later called Mexico in the early sixteenth century. Despite recorded forms of landownership and organized land tenure, they frequently treated indigenous lands as vacant, occupying them for their own use and employing a system of forced native labor.[5] Additionally, due to contact with Europeans, indigenous communities lost large numbers of people due to health epidemics throughout the colonial period, oftentimes leading land to be unused or vacant, leaving it vulnerable to claims by Spaniards. While native populations began to recover in numbers in the seventeenth century, they lacked the political and economic power to reclaim land that had belonged to their ancestors. Through the process of progressive land loss and reduced land access, native people were largely stripped of their ability to provide for themselves, resulting in the need for wage work, either on Spanish-owned haciendas, or via migration to other regions or cities (Altman, Cline, and Pescador 2003; Borah 1983; Cline 1986; Lockhart 1969).

Several centuries after initial colonial contact, indigenous landholding was further stripped away through the process of declaring Mexican nationhood. Although the war for Mexican independence from 1810 to 1821 was initiated on behalf of the poor, it was also rooted in a push for a more individualist ideology around landownership. Before independence from Spain, both the Catholic Church and indigenous communities held land in communal or institutional ownership. Under the Spanish Crown, indigenous communities that still held communal land had their land rights somewhat legally protected. After Mexico gained independence in 1821, that protection was lost, leaving such communities even more vulnerable to seizure of their land by powerful elites (Brading 1991; Harvey 2000).

Despite indigenous loss of communal land rights, the guerrilla factions that won the war for independence remained entrenched in a broader long-term struggle for peasant land rights. Over the course of the nineteenth century, the concentration of lands and power of the hacienda owners only increased, leaving a country of dispossessed peasants ready to fight for land access. Hacienda expansion during this period was complex and varied by region. Generally, the flat lowland areas were more profitable for expansion, whereas the central and southern highland regions were less ecologically desirable for such colonization. Many indigenous communities were able to resist foreign agrarian development in these areas (Assies 2008).

Loss of indigenous and peasant land, and the poverty that it caused among the majority of the Mexican population, eventually came to a boiling point. The Mexican Revolution of 1910–1920 was largely a response to this widespread unrest and inequality, which had come to a climax under the thirty-five-year rule of president Porfirio Díaz. Under Díaz, haciendas were further consolidated and an agro-export economy was established, including the sale of millions of reportedly unused hectares to US companies. During this time, 87 percent of rural land was held by 0.2 percent of the landowners (ibid.).

Peasant leaders, most famously, Emilio Zapata and Francisco "Pancho" Villa, fought for land redistribution as one of the primary goals of the revolution. Zapata rallied under the slogans *Tierra y libertad* (land and liberty) and *La tierra es de quien la trabaja* (the land belongs to those who work it). They struggled for the return of hacienda lands to landless peasants, although the call for a return to communal landholdings was not universal throughout the country (ibid.). While Article 27 of the 1917 Mexican Constitution directly called for the dividing of haciendas and the redistribution of property to the landless, it was not until President Lázaro Cárdenas passed the 1934 Agrarian Code that significant land reform came to pass. Major progress began in 1935. Cárdenas worked with peasant groups to dismantle the hacienda system, redistributing over 20 million hectares through the development and institutionalization of the *ejido*, or communal land, system. By 1940, almost half of all arable land was part of the ejido sector. By the 1980s, around 28,000 ejidos, including 3.5 million agrarian worker-owners, had been created through agrarian reform. These holdings, while communally held and restricted in terms of sale to private individuals, were not strictly for subsistence production. Ejidos produced food for commercial sale as well as for their own community-owner consumption (ibid.; Keen and Haynes 2012).

The dividing of lands was not universal, though, and some powerful large-scale private landowners continued to coexist alongside the communal land structure, creating a stark economic divide. Although under Cárdenas the ejidos were supported through credit, price guarantees, and infrastructure, in the long run, the parcels of the ejido system proved too small and of too poor quality for many producers to economically survive. Once political favor returned to the side of private landownership, smallholder ejidos struggled to compete with industrial agrarian export production. This ultimately led to a bifurcation of rural spaces and the rural economy between the communal ejido holdings and highly intensive private commercial production. Though the ejido holdings grew progressively through the 1980s, not all *ejiditarios* were able to make a living from the land. Much of the redistributed land was not arable or productive, and many supplemented their income as wageworkers in agriculture and other sectors, including by migrating to the United States. Some ejido lands were rented out for profit as people no longer wanted to farm it themselves (Assies 2008).

Although some scholars have argued that the history of the common ejido experience has forged an identity of resistance to global free market forces and a communal land ethic (Eisenstadt 2009; Teubal 2009), through my interviews I found that immigrant farmers have a mixed interest in communal farming. Of the small number committed to cooperative farming, they tend to have work experience outside farm labor, and usually in some kind of social movement organizing. For most, when I asked about working with other immigrants, farmworkers, or even family members outside their nuclear family, as co-owners of land or businesses, they had an immediate and direct response that they preferred to work alone. Some cited failed experiences working on communal projects in Mexico and in the United States, although none addressed the ejido system directly.

The ejido project was formally ended in 1991 by President Carlos Salinas de Gortari, who reformed the Mexican Constitution's Article 27, which had obligated the government to redistribute land, and limited the division of ejido lands or sale to private owners or nonlaborers. Instead, under the justification of increasing productivity and flows of capital, President Salinas worked toward strengthening individual property rights and engaging Mexico further in the global neoliberal economy. Reforming Article 27 meant that foreign and private investors could now purchase ejido lands, reversing protections for Mexican smallholder landownership and peasant livelihoods. In addition to doing away with government land distribution objectives, the president further liberalized Mexico's agrarian sector, cutting state-funded subsidies, guaranteed prices for crops, and crop insurance (Assies 2008; Nock 2000; Teubal 2009; Vázquez-Castillo 2004).

Despite these shifts in policy, the transition from communal to private ownership has been slow, given that ejido owners have traditionally had few opportunities for income outside the agricultural sector, and most ejido lands have limited viability for commercial production, while the lands continue to have social and economic significance, thereby outweighing the appeal of individual tenure. Additionally, although the program was formally ended, some ejidos still exist without formal government sanctions.

The final push in undoing communal land tenure and peasants' ability to subsist off the land came with a transnational agreement between Mexico, the United States, and Canada. In 1994, overlapping with the final dismantling of the ejido system, President Salinas signed NAFTA. This arrangement further solidified the liberalization of the Mexican agrarian economy and prioritization of global free trade, resulting in massive migration to the United States.[6]

By reducing barriers to trade and tariffs on imports from the United States, NAFTA allowed the agricultural economy to be deluged by foodstuffs key to the Mexican agrarian economy. The cheap production of maize (corn) and beans by US farmers subsidized by the US government flooded the local markets, making it impossible for small-scale Mexican farmers to compete. NAFTA acted as a powerful linchpin in the already-changing Mexican rural landscape from that of mixed commercial and subsistence production to heavy export production. Unemployment and increased rural poverty among small-scale farmers were direct consequences of the agreement (Martin 2003). In particular, out-migration has been highest from Mexico's corn-producing regions (Nadal 2002). Immediately following the signing of NAFTA, corn prices in Mexico fell $160 per ton. At the same time, imports of US corn to Mexico increased by twenty times their previous level. Over that same period, the number of Mexican corn producers declined by one-third of its pre-1994 level (Relinger 2010).

Additionally, as farmers were forced to compete with cheap commodities from the United States and Canada, many started using synthetic pesticides and fertilizers for the first time. Carlos, a farmer in New York introduced in chapter 4, recounted, "It's funny, you know, where we're from at least, we didn't get introduced to commercial fertilizer and chemicals until NAFTA." As I discuss in the previous chapter, Carlos lamented his family's use of synthetic additions and loss of more traditional farming practices, which he blames on the competition from US imports.

NAFTA also created new spaces for continued foreign investment in tourism and industry. This foreign funding, which came largely from the United States, fueled the opening of factories employing low-wage Mexican labor. These foreign developments perpetuated the displacement of the ejido system by urbanizing the countryside, replacing food-producing rural livelihoods with industries whose profits were not reinvested in the local regions (Vázquez-Castillo 2004). This shift has caused a massive migration of former peasant farmers, generally from the south to the north of Mexico as well as across the border to the United States, looking for work in industrial agriculture, manufacturing, and service industries.

Many farmers I interviewed noted how the depressed rural economy in Mexico pressured them to look outside their hometowns and states to other regions and eventually across the border for work. While most farmers did not mention NAFTA directly, they spoke about poverty more generally, and the challenges of farming with low resources and high competition. This rural poverty, creating an impossible context to successfully farm and feed one's family, has led to the disempowerment of peasant farmers and a mass exodus of farmers from Mexico to the United States looking for work as laborers in the fields.

After leaving their own communities, culture, and lands, immigrant laborers migrate to the United States to work in agriculture and other industries, under often-exploitative conditions. They bring these experiences of displacement, migration, and labor with them as they start their own farms and become new farmers. As they break through the racialized and hierarchical structure of US farming, it is this experience as immigrants and workers that motivates them to find a new place on the aforementioned agricultural ladder. It is also this experience that positions them as potential actors in resisting dominant agrifood power structures as they bring a distinct connection to land as well their own agrarian knowledge and labor with them to the United States.

Self-Direction, Freedom, and the Love of Farming

For farmers I interviewed, food production and a connection to the land is a tradition that has spanned generations. As evidenced from the Mexican history detailed in the section above, the peasant class in Mexico has spent hundreds of years resisting its dispossession from its land-based livelihoods. I have found that this resistance has never stopped, although for immigrants in the United States, it takes on a different form as they work toward reclaiming land and labor across geographic and cultural divisions.

Farming is not an economically rational choice for those wishing to go into business. The work is temporal. The profits are based on increasingly erratic weather patterns, and the learning curve and investment in improving the land are steep. Instead, for the immigrant farmers I interviewed, the decision to farm was about a particular kind of freedom—a freedom to control one's time and labor, and also to live in a way that is more connected to agrarian values. Farmers' search for this freedom connects their lives in the United States to their previous ones in Mexico. In their eyes, they never stopped being farmers; instead, they were temporarily disconnected from the resources or means to practice farming. As scholars of the food sovereignty movement have identified, it is this connection to food production as a livelihood and cultural practice that differentiates this agrifood movement from industrial agriculture or standard agribusiness (Patel 2009).

The drive for independence was an overwhelming motivation among farmers in my research. Although farmers lose the relative stability of a paycheck, they gain the ability to determine their own activities and schedule, in addition to increased control over their families' food access. This finding reflects Wells's study of Mexican workers turned strawberry growers and sharecroppers in the 1970s and 1980s. In her work, Wells (1984, 18) found that the possibility of "self-direction" was a huge motivating factor for starting their businesses.

The concept of a stable income is relative for farmworkers. Their actual income as new farmers in the United States varies, although most say they are still struggling financially. Farmers told me they do not make much more in take-home income than they did as farmworkers, and some say they actually make less. The majority of farmers interviewed had formerly worked as seasonal workers, meaning they were hired by a farm owner or contractor by the season, providing them no long-term financial stability. Some moved from region to region with harvest cycles, while others stayed in one area and pieced together other jobs for the winter. At the very least, though, those hired by honest employers could trust that if they worked a full day, they would be paid for it.[7] In contrast, as owners of their own farms, there is no guarantee they will sell their product, or that a drought or plague won't wipe out their crop.

Trinidad, a mixed fruit and vegetable farmer, immigrated from Jalisco to Virginia about thirty years ago. He owns approximately sixty acres, which he acquired slowly throughout the years. His farm was one of the largest in my study. Trinidad has been farming his own land for almost twenty years with his wife, children, and elderly parents. When I asked him about the financial instability of owning a farm, he described the experience: "You're not guaranteed money at the end of the week. You could work pretty much sixty hours a week, and then at the end of the week you're like, 'Where's my money?'"

The sacrifice of a relatively stable income is obviously a huge risk to take, especially for those who have little or no financial cushion. Yet as they leave behind their day jobs and their small but more dependable income, they gain a sense of independence and freedom from the daily grind of a hired worker.

Sara and her husband, Ernesto, both introduced in chapter 4, rent land from Viva Farms, the nonprofit incubator farming organization in Washington's Skagit Valley introduced in the first chapter. The couple grows strawberries and raspberries for regional farmers markets, and corn and beans for their own family's consumption. Sara echoed Ricardo's sentiment above. Her experience as a worker and the opportunity for the freedom to create her own timeline was a motivating factor for starting her own business. "If you are a worker, you have a set schedule," she explains. "When you are an owner, you have to come earlier, but you can leave whenever you want. For me, it is very good to be a business owner, not to have schedule, and not having to say that you have to leave and have the manager

Figure 5.2
Senaida Vela of Arado Farm next to her raspberry bushes in Washington State.

be mad at you. Sometimes, if you need to go to the doctor, the people in charge don't want to let you go."

Yet farmworkers need not stay in agriculture in order to own their own business. Even nonimmigrant farmers struggle economically in an industry known to be unforgiving to small business owners. In each interview I asked farmers, "Why farming? Why not some other kind of business where it is easier to make a living?" I was consistently reminded that for these farmers, cultivating food was something more important than a moneymaking enterprise. The choice to start a farm instead of another kind of operation is an intentional one, with deep meaning for those who choose it. While Sara and Ricardo only grow a few crops for market, their access to land where they choose to grow crops for their own consumption means that their family not only has improved food security but also increased control over the source and quality of that food, reflecting key food sovereignty principles. For the farmers I interviewed, the practices of growing their own food in addition to food for sale, while using their chosen approaches, was what made farming worth it.

Sara's husband, Ernesto, explained the connection between his experience as a farmer and farmworker to his business today. "I think that we who love the fields, we came from the fields. I think, personally, that's what attracts us—we know how to do it, we have practice, we can adapt, we get to know the products, we get the opportunity to have experience."

As I discussed in the last chapter, beyond knowing how to farm, immigrant farmers' experience as small-scale farmers in Mexico plays a major role in their farming decisions in the United States, particularly the motivation to stay in agriculture rather than move on to another profession. Although others acknowledge the desire to move away from farming, as Victoria, introduced in chapter 4, explains, after leaving and trying other things, many return to a land-based livelihood. "That always happens in farming, you know? You grew up on a farm, and then when you move to the States, you get tired of working on farms. I've seen this a lot. They take a little break and they always come back to where they started. So I think that happened to me."

Of course, for many, staying in agriculture simply makes the most sense. They have always worked in agriculture and know growing food better than anything else. José, a Virginia farmer mentioned in previous chapters, told me, "Why? Because we're back to the same. ... We didn't study. We could do something else, but this is what we know how to do and we like it. I like it. And ... I like to do it. For fun? No. To live, for my parents, to spend, to eat."

Returning to farming as a producer, after being a worker, allows him to reclaim the labor he has always done. It is simultaneously practical, based on his skills and knowledge base, and part of fulfilling his identity as a farmer.

Diego is a middle-aged farmer who lives in a house on five acres of rented land on the Central Coast of California. I asked him why he didn't simply grow strawberries, the most profitable regional crop, like most other farmers in the area. He responded, "They do it for the money, I do it for the freedom." Diego related his choice to grow a diversity of crops to the "freedom" of farming. As a former farmworker struggling to establish a plot of land, the ability to make his own choices as to how to utilize his own labor was reflected in practices that represent his past experience in contrast to those being dictated to him. This kind of autonomy and "freedom" is a driving force behind the ideals of food sovereignty: the notion that farmers should once again be empowered to control their own labor and decision making.

Victoria proudly describes the variety of plants she grows as well as her practice of saving seeds. By saving seeds year to year for planting, she maintains agrodiversity as well as avoids purchasing seeds from industrial agricultural companies.

> I have two kinds of Chinese broccoli, cauliflowers, mustard, different kinds of lettuce. I have many different kinds of stuff. In Mexico, people use epazote, a plant called *ruda*, *apali*, *peicha*, and all of that. A lot of people look for me because of that. A lot of people know me and they look for me because they know that I have different stuff. … Sometimes, Asian people bring me seeds. They tell me to leave one or two plants so they can produce seeds, and I can plant again next year, and that's what I do. I save different kinds of seeds. I don't even have them labeled because I'm the only one who knows it. My husband doesn't know anything.

Seed saving exemplifies a key tenant of food sovereignty: to keep a closed resource loop as much as possible in order to reduce dependence on agribusiness firms, therefore democratizing control over the food system. The industrial food system ties farmers to particular practices, crops, and market relationships. By seeking sovereignty over their food production and consumption, immigrant farmers are empowered to make their own decisions concerning what crop varieties to plant and eat. While they are limited in how much they can afford to disengage from industrial-scale agribusiness as a whole, they are still engaging in creating oppositional agrarian spaces (Trauger 2017).

Mateo, a farmer in California introduced in chapter 4, acknowledged that no matter how much experience one has, farming is always a struggle. Yet, at the end of the day, he told me, it is important to love what you do and feel committed to the practice. Mateo was part of one of the first graduating classes from ALBA and is focused on making a profit, but is clear

Figure 5.3
Dried beans sold by a Latino/a farmer at a farmers market in California.

that concentrating on income has to be in balance with a way of life that fulfills his farming goals. "I like the life [of a farmer]. I don't necessarily recommend it. You have to love agriculture. You need to love farming more than you love money. One of the first things is that you have to love this. You can't do it for the money—that is part of farming. You get married two times—you are married to farming. You have to love it."

When I asked Mateo why he grows mixed vegetables instead of berries, like the majority of farmers in his region, he responded similarly to Diego above. It is more than an economic venture; it is also about a way of living—a theme I explored more in chapter 4. He told me, "It is more expensive to grow strawberries, more labor. Vegetables are a more open market—people eat more of them. It costs less, less stress, less technical [than berries]. Vegetables are more peaceful, it is less pressure. Less difficult for me. I earn less for vegetables, but it is a better life for me."

While profit is important, spending his time growing food in a way that feels satisfying is a large part of why he stays in agriculture. It is not simply

Figure 5.4
Diverse varieties of greens on a Latino/a farm in Virginia's "Black Dirt" region.

a business, but also a way of life. Now that he has control over his own labor and time, he wants to spend it in a way that feels valuable to him, not only to reproduce the same system he labored in as a farmworker. This reclaiming of his own time and labor along with agricultural space represents a shift away from an imposed industrial food system, and toward one where immigrants and workers are deciding what to produce as well as consume. As he points out, though, the way he chooses to farm can require more labor, and that labor is often expected of farmers' families and close community. The complexities of labor and tensions between capitalist and alternative forms of production is the topic to which I now turn.

Tensions of Labor, Scale, and Sustainability

As I have discussed throughout this book, immigrant farmers in this study generally prefer to maintain mid- to small-scale production, including diverse crop systems, and direct and local sales of their products. For immigrant farmers, maintaining a relatively small-scale farm and avoiding industrial growing techniques, such as monocropping and nonorganic inputs, is clearly related to sustaining a primarily family-based workforce. As I reviewed in chapter 4, the choice to not use noxious pesticides and insecticides was partially motivated by the fact that they regularly have family present on the farm. Conversely, it is only by remaining smaller scale that they can avoid hiring nonfamily labor.

Wells's (1996) research shows that Mexican farmers in the United States (in comparison to Japanese and white farmers) were more likely to emphasize the importance of family labor as a key to farming success. She credits this difference largely to Mexican farmers' lack of economic resources and the simultaneous wealth of available family labor. Close family networks are a form of social capital that immigrants hold, in contrast to economic capital. Her findings build on Alexander Chayanov's work (1986), arguing that family labor is crucial to the traditional peasant economy. I saw similar reasoning for hiring family over nonfamily labor, as relatives were available to them, and family connectivity was a cultural value that they aimed to reinforce on their farms.

Family labor, however, does not imply an inherently better or more equitable labor system, and by no means ensures labor justice on the farm. Research has shown that smaller-scale and organic production similarly do not guarantee farm equality (Shreck, Getz, and Feenstra 2006). Family relations vary, and unequal gender relations can be amplified in a family business, particularly an agricultural one (Feldman and Welsh 1995; Reed et al. 1999; Riley 2009). While some farms' laborers consisted of a married couple and their children, others included cousins, siblings, or parents of the farmers. As in any family situation, I can only assume there were tensions between family members concerning the division of labor and material goods. Although I did not interview individual members of the same family alone (I did interview many couples together), nor did I ask directly about gendered divisions of labor or sharing of profits, I commonly observed shared homes, meals, vehicles, and other material resources among family members. Unlike hired labor, family members were typically not paid hourly wages, and farm resources were considered those belonging to the farmer and their families, and treated as such.

Some farmers interviewed hire nonfamily workers at busy times in the season. Others are starting to feel the pressure to scale up as they struggle to find local markets. Another group of immigrant farmers, as I discussed earlier, already farm using more conventional practices and regularly hire nonfamily work crews. For those who already hire nonfamily laborers, they employ other immigrants from the regions they migrated from, such as Jalisco and Michoacán, while others hire newer immigrants from more southerly Mexican states (more heavily populated by indigenous people), such as Oaxaca and Chiapas.[8] Frequently, employees were from a mix of states and regions, as the worker population largely reflected the general immigrant streams in various locations of the United States.

As for how they may or may not replicate their own labor conditions when, or if, they scale up their farm production and hire nonfamily labor, it is hard to extrapolate. Although many farmers were willing to let me talk to their workers, be they family or hired labor, I was not in a position to get a fully transparent perspective from those laborers, who were introduced to me by their boss. From their own perspectives as employers, immigrant farmers asserted that given their experiences as workers, they treat their hired labor well, and better than they were treated. Many argued that this was due to their understanding of what it is like to be in the employees' position.

Samuel, a farmer in Minnesota mentioned in chapter 3, is married, but his wife and four teenage children are still living in Mexico, so he employs his brother as well as a few other hired laborers. "One of the most significant expenses here in the United States is labor. It is not that we don't want to pay people, but we need to have a big operation to be able to pay them. You end up doing most of it with the help of friends and family." Samuel was clear about the need to respect and recognize the contributions of those who work for him, yet honest about his limitations in paying them well for the time they provided, saying, "I think that when you start from the bottom, you understand the problems and the process. I think that it is important to realize that if you grew up in the fields, you know the conditions. You also know when people treated you good or bad. You need to treat your workers well; they are the ones who are helping you."

As he explains, from his former experience as a hired worker, he takes seriously his own dependence on his laborers and aims to be a better employer. Rodolfo, an orchardist in Washington mentioned in chapter 3, made a similar argument. Unlike many immigrant farmers, he has experience working in cities as well as on farms, and speaks English proficiently. He was able to buy his land after many years working on orchards in the region. He also maintained that his experience as a worker leads him to treat his workers better.

> When you are an owner, you have to pay somebody to do the job. When you are a worker, you have in your head that no one is going to be better than you, and you have an idea of how much you want to make in a day. You know what you expect from each worker, [and] you can treat the workers better if you are an owner. … We've been lucky that the people who help keep coming back season after season, and I think it's because we treat them well. … We offer them drinks like Gatorade or sodas during their breaks, and that makes people happy. During the season, we make like a family party because it's the same people. I think that because we were workers and because we would have like for people to treat us like that, we treat workers well.

As Rodolfo states, he believes that because they have experience as workers, they are inclined to treat their own workers better. Many even pride themselves on their treatment of workers. Since they are also immigrants and speak the same language as their workers, unlike many other employers, they see themselves as more understanding of workers' needs.

Antonio immigrated in 2001 from Puebla to the Hudson Valley. Antonio learned how to farm from his grandfather and father in Mexico, and credits growing up on his family's farm as his primary training in agriculture. Since 2009, Antonio has been renting his land from a neighboring larger-scale farm and grows mostly for farmers markets as well as a few wholesalers. He farms primarily with his wife and one of their aunts, who also lives with them. They hire a few nonfamily workers. "A couple of people come when they have time." He describes their situation: "They are working, but I am not trying to push them like you have to finish this. You know, take your time. They can take a little break or drink water, use the restroom, do whatever you have to do. … Some guys who I talk to, you know, I am Mexican/Latino, so I talk to them, and they say they [other employers] have them like slaves."

Actions like offering water, giving breaks, or hosting a party might sound like small gestures or trite offerings of friendliness to gain the loyalty of workers. Certainly, it is not unique among farmers for immigrant employers to make efforts to build their personal relationships with their workers. Yet it is common for farmworkers to have worked under conditions where basic labor laws such as providing water breaks were not enforced. Antonio, quoted above, described the wage theft that is common in his region. He told me that although the minimum wage "now is eight plus. Most of the people [farmers], they don't like to pay $9, whatever the minimum is. They pay you $5.15."[9] Clearly the changes they are making are not revolutionary, nor are they significantly challenging owner-worker relations. Yet as employers, they see themselves as providing their employees a better work environment and decent, or at least legal, wages.

For many, being friends with their workers was a point of pride. Gerardo, a recent immigrant from Oaxaca who was introduced in chapter 3, farms in California. He talked of respect for his workers and the ways in which he valued their opinions on things from appropriate weather for working to the daily farm schedule. "I feel so happy because my workers feel comfortable with me, they feel like really open, we share opinions, and I asked them things like, 'What do you guys think about the weather? Is it too hot? What do you guys think about working these hours?' I work with them because even if they are workers, they have something to say, and you have to respect their opinions."

Because of their smaller scale, farmers are generally working alongside any workers they have hired. Even on the largest farms I visited, the farmers prided themselves on being in the fields with their workers on a daily basis. Jesus, a farmer who owns orchards in central Washington and was first introduced in chapter 3, describes the difference between his own work practices and those of US-born farmers, and how being an immigrant and former farmworker affects his relationship with his workers:

> Most of the first-generation [immigrant] farmers are over there looking at things, making sure they are done the right way, the way they're supposed to. The guys who have been there for a long time or who inherit it, they don't seem to care one way or the other, they just want that income to keep coming. ... A lot of the farmers who are not out there, they don't care about a relationship with the workers, they just come and tell their manager things, and that's it. They go and do whatever they do during the day.

He even pointed out that when he is working with the crew, he will be mistaken for a worker himself. He laughed as he told me the story of being unrecognizable as the boss to new employees since he blends in with the other workers due to his race.

> A lot of times, maybe half a dozen times, we get new workers, and we get people to help us all the time transporting equipment, and this and that. ... There was a guy taking equipment back and forward, and doing other things. After the fourth day, a couple of the guys who came to help us work asked the guy who I had as the boss [crew manager]: "How come the owner doesn't come in?" The guy said, "What do you mean, he doesn't come in?" "Yeah, he just comes and goes in the truck and never stops." "He is not the owner; he is just a worker. The owner is this one." That has happened half a dozen times. ... They think I'm just part of the crew.

Farmers' perceptions of their relationship to their employees varies, though, as some admit that camaraderie with their workers is more about strategy than friendship. I met Alonso, a stout middle-aged man, at a farmers market outside Seattle. His entire family, including the children, worked as migrant workers when he was growing up. His father started their farm in eastern Washington in the 1970s, although Alonso continued to work off the family farm to make extra money until he was an adult himself. When I asked how he thought his relationship with his workers differs from employers without his experience, he told me, "I think it is probably a totally different relationship. First, being Mexican and getting minority workers to work with me, I try to make all my workers my friends—that's the key if you want them to care. You can tell them, 'Hey that's not going to work. Or do this.' Being friends with you, makes it better. I think my relationship with them is better than, I would say, an employer who has sixty or seventy guys out there who he doesn't even know."

Yet closer relationships also create new challenges. As employers who share similar class backgrounds, experiences, and language, and are often in the same social networks as their employees, they struggle with how to determine boundaries. Rodolfo puts it this way,

> It's difficult when you don't know how to distinguish friendship from work. Most workers are our friends. We have established a friendship, but they've started to distinguish when the friendship ends and when the work begins. You have to be more concrete on what you want and establish boundaries "I started paying you, and unfortunately you are my worker. You'll be my friend when I stop paying you." You can do that. Those who don't understand that, they are still my friends, but they don't work for me anymore.

Others were more direct about the fact that treating their workers well was more about the general procedure of doing business legally. Miguel, a Washington farmer originally from Oaxaca who was introduced in chapter 4, never completed elementary school. His oldest son, who was educated in the United States, now manages the business and marketing of his farm. Most of his farm work is done by family labor. He has seven adult children who all are part of the business in some way. But during the harvest season, he hires some nonfamily employees. He says this of his relationship with them: "If somebody breaks their foot, somebody gets injured by a tractor or a machine, that's also difficult. That's why I organize meetings with the people who are working with me. I talk to them about being careful. 'Take your time. Be careful when cars come near. Take breaks even if I'm not here.' Because the law is the law."

Miguel was honest that although he wanted to be kind and generous with his workers, he also feels obligated to do so by the law. In that way, he is like any other employer: following the rules regarding employee treatment is important to sustaining his business, and is not just a matter of being kind or generous.

Unfortunately, given their limited profits as small-scale farmers with limited access to markets, they are constrained in their ability to provide higher wages and benefits, such as health care and sick leave. Even with the best intentions, should they be assumed, immigrant farmers are caught in the same economic system as other farmers, competing with global industrial production and struggling to make ends meet. Andres in California describes feeling stuck in his position as an employer who would like to do more, but can't because of his limited profits.

> I didn't like how they treated me in my other job; they wanted me to always move fast, and they didn't pay well. Here, I tried to help them as much as I can. Sometimes I can't help them a lot because I'm not earning much, but I try to do my best. Sometimes just by bringing water or soda, you make them happy. That is something that I saw at my previous job, because they didn't bring me like a soda or anything. I see that sometimes when you bring them something, they are very grateful. Sometimes I make a barbeque. I try to help them in what I can.

Certainly, moving up the ladder from farmworker to farm owner does not solve the problem of labor exploitation or structural inequality in any way. Although farmers may want to treat their workers better than they were treated, they are challenged by the same market squeezes and struggle to profit as other farmers.

Conclusion

Repossessing their own labor and the means to produce food empowers workers, as they strive to advance their class status against enormous odds. As I have discussed in this chapter, immigrant farmers have roots in peasant and indigenous communities in Mexico, who have been struggling against the process of dispossession from their land for centuries. For those who have relocated to the United States, starting their own farm is a process of reclaiming the means of production, their own labor, and some form of sovereignty over the food system, albeit on a small scale.

Reclaiming food production for immigrant farmers includes prioritizing family involvement on the farm, as farming is as much about a way of life as it is a business. Those who have succeeded in re-creating the traditional version of the family farm prioritize food consumption and a safe environment for their loved ones, as I discussed in earlier chapters. Those priorities, along with their stated goals of finding independence and freedom from industrial agricultural spaces as well as practices, reflect the core principles of the food sovereignty movement, which may offer potential opportunities for broader alliances and engagements among immigrant farmers and other formerly dispossessed groups of farmers.

Yet contrary to the ideals of the food sovereignty movement, and the stated personal values of the farmers themselves, economic realities may force them to reproduce their own labored experience by hiring nonfamily workers full or part time. Although their experience as workers informs their relationship with and understanding of the workers they hire, it in no way guarantees improved wages and benefits for workers or a more just food system overall. As one farmer made clear when I asked him if more immigrants owning farms would change the circumstances for workers, it simply "depends on the farmer. There are Mexicans who feel sorry for their workers and will pay them well, but not all of us have the same feelings. There are farmers who are going to say, 'I don't care about people, it's just work and that's it.'"

As far as shifting class relations, the workers who are able to start their own farms and join the owner class are just as vulnerable to market pressures to save on labor costs as any other farmer. Agrarian capitalism creates a labor hierarchy, and although immigrant farmers challenge this hierarchy from the perspective of race, ethnicity, and citizenship, as long as they are competing in the global food marketplace, they are not in a position to structurally resist it. While immigrant farmers are good examples of cracks in the deeply racialized and class-based agrarian system today, they are still forced to reproduce this system to survive.

In order for a sustained resistance to these structures to change the daily pressures farmers feel, the broader alternative farming community, including farmers, activists, and consumers, must recognize the particular challenges that immigrant farmers face. Potentially the conceptual umbrella of food sovereignty could provide a structure to support immigrant farmers in the context of such challenges. If such a movement is to make deeper structural change to our food system, particularly in the United States, practical solutions must include creating incentives for white farmers to pass on agricultural land to their workers, strengthening market access for smaller-scale and more agroecologically focused farmers, and creating ways to make farming more profitable without squeezing workers even further. Without such systematic changes and strong alliances to specifically support them, it is unclear how immigrants and other farmers of color will maintain their small-scale and alternative practices—a topic I address in the conclusion.

6   The Rain Falls for Every Farmer: Growing Ecological and Social Diversity

If the sun comes out for everybody, why have envy? It comes out for everybody. It comes out for whites, for Latinos, for Japanese, for everybody. The sun does not discriminate. The rain falls for every farmer.

—Fernandez

Fernandez, a Mixteco man in his early thirties from Oaxaca, farms on a rented half acre in Washington State. I spoke with him while sitting at a worn picnic table on a sunny May day, adjacent to the land he had just started cultivating at the Viva Farms incubator project in the Skagit Valley. His positivity and excitement was contagious. He spoke of his two young children as his inspiration to farm. "If I don't teach my kids [farming], then they won't teach their kids." He was filled with joy when he spoke of the opportunity he had been given to grow on his own after many years laboring as a farmworker. Yet a dark cloud seemed to cover his face when I asked him about his experience as a farm laborer in the United States, and the way his boss treated him and other workers. He told me, "They only think about squeezing the worker, and when you are old, they kick you out." For that reason, because he knows there is no advancement as a worker, only rejection when his body wears out, he decided to work two jobs, farmer and farmworker, day and night, to create more opportunity for his family.

Fernandez was painfully aware that the chances of his success as a farmer were not in his favor. He also told me, "White people have advantages up here, and the Latinos do not. A white person can go to the bank and get a loan; they can open up the market. There are always barriers for the Latinos." Yet he continued day in and day out, because as he says, the sun still comes out, despite these inequities. In my short time speaking

with Fernandez, he articulated both the most hopeful and sobering findings I have observed throughout this study. While many more farmworkers are succeeding at harnessing the power and promise of the sun than
most people would expect, immigrant farmers struggle to equitably access
resources and opportunities as compared to other farmers in the United
States, despite the experience, knowledge, and incredible commitment to
agriculture that they bring with them. Additionally, the structure of the
US agricultural market and production system promotes as well as benefits
industrial agriculture, as opposed to alternative growing practices and marketing strategies, putting these farmers at a further disadvantage given their
largely nonconventional approaches. A vivid conclusion I came to while
doing this research is that for immigrant farmers to succeed, actors in the
alternative food system must recognize immigrant farmers as playing an
integral role in alternative food production. Immigrant farmers will fully
benefit from the new spaces being created for other small-scale, diversified,
and low-input producers only when alternative food movement actors start
to proactively recognize the work they are already doing.

The Hidden Role of Immigrant Farmers in Alternative Food Systems

Immigrant farmers are committed to approaches that could be classified as
alternative food practices, yet as immigrant farmers of color, they are commonly overlooked in the story of local and alternative food. Immigrant
farmers and other farmers of color specifically struggle to gain access to
the affluent white consumers they need to make their businesses thrive, as
markets and alternative food institutions are dominated by farmers who
are more likely to resonate culturally with food buyers and managers. In
addition to the evidence presented in this book, many other scholars have
observed an overwhelming trend among alternative food activists and
actors to disregard race and racial politics in their spaces as well as narratives,
including farmers markets, community-supported agriculture boosters, student activists, food security groups, food purchasing coops, and alternative
farming coalitions (Alkon 2012, 2008; Alkon and McCullen 2011; Guthman 2008a, 2008b; Slocum 2008; Reynolds and Cohen 2016). I believe this
is part of the reason why the immigrant farmers I spoke with expressed
little interest in being involved with alternative food movements—they
do not see their own challenges and priorities reflected in the narratives

and actions of dominant movement actors. I hope that recommendations coming out of this book foster more understanding of Latino/a and other immigrant and farmers of color, creating more inclusive agrifood organizations and spaces on a national scale, and therefore inspiring more farmers to identify with such movements.

Despite these exclusions, much progress is being made in alternative agrifood movements, as activists, consumers, and farmers create new coalitions to address racism in the food system more broadly. Social issues such as labor injustice, immigration, and sexual violence are being faced head-on, as they intersect with the racial politics of food production, processing, sales, and service. Food justice and food sovereignty coalitions are bringing farmers of color together with food movement activists and consumers, and in doing so, changing what the image of an alternative farmer is expected to look like (see, among others, Alkon 2007; Koohafkan and Altieri 2016; Bowens 2015b; McCutcheon 2013; Morales 2011; Reynolds and Cohen 2016; Trauger 2017; Wittman, Desmarais, and Wiebe 2010). Popular media and organizational blogs highlighting alternative food systems work, such as *Civil Eats, Food Tank,* and *YES! Magazine,* as well as groups like the National Sustainable Agriculture Coalition are advocating for a more inclusive food system and underscoring the work of farmers of color (see Bowens 2015a; National Sustainable Agriculture Coalition 2018; Penniman 2017; Urdanivia 2018).

In particular, African American farmers and agricultural groups are gaining national recognition for highlighting the historical contributions of farmers of color. New farming projects centering farmers of color are growing in rural areas such as upstate New York and southwest Georgia as well as urban centers such as Washington, DC, and Detroit.[1] They are building on the legacy of black activists who focused on alternative forms of agriculture, such as Fannie Lou Hamer, a civil rights organizer who turned to cooperative farming as part of black liberation, and George Washington Carver, a botanist and professor who encouraged rotating crops for soil cultivation (Lee 2000; McCutcheon 2013; Paynter 2018). These farms are explicitly addressing not only food insecurity in their communities but also the broader issues of land reparations and food sovereignty by reclaiming the means to produce food for themselves.

Yet the pressure to scale up, decrease crop diversity, and hire low-wage nonfamily workers is always looming, as farmers struggle to maintain an alternative form of farming and also stay true to their original motivations to start their own farming business. Despite their success at starting their own businesses, all the farmers I interviewed expressed challenges to sustaining the scale and form they prefer. Many are struggling to sell the products they already grow. Instead of aspiring to scale up their production, they conveyed frustration at the lack of outlets for what they were already growing.

The question looms, notwithstanding the fact that immigrant farmers are making considerable contributions to alternative food and farming systems, will they be able to survive pressures from the market to shift to more industrial methods or will they persist as alternative farmers? In the section below, I make some specific recommendations regarding creating a more inclusive food and farming system—one where immigrant farmers can thrive and continue to contribute to growing alternative food networks.

Improving Institutional and Technical Support

Despite being marginalized by state and other institutional authorities, immigrant farmers are still rising in numbers, and drawing on their own agrarian knowledge and norms to preserve their agrifood traditions and practices. These farmers are cultivating in a way that contributes to local economies and ecosystems as well as creating a more culturally diverse populace of US farm owners. Although most farmers I spoke with are currently making their businesses work, many waver on the edge of economic stability. Without institutional support and acknowledgment of these differences in agrarian practice, their farm businesses may not survive in the long term.

While conducting this research, I encountered numerous positive examples of shifting institutional culture, where individuals and organizations were actively broadening their knowledge base and skill sets in order to create specific resources along with accessible spaces for immigrants and other farmers of color. Organizations that I have discussed throughout the book, including the Small Farms Program at Washington State University, Crossroads Community Food Network in Takoma Park, Maryland, incubator programs such as Viva Farms in Mount Vernon, Washington, ALBA in Salinas, California, and the Latino Economic Development Center in Saint Paul, Minnesota, among others, are excellent models of established groups that are creating opportunities and support systems for workers to make the challenging transition to farm ownership.

Immigrant farmers are seeking institutional homes outside agricultural centers as well. Some Latino/a communities are looking for ways to support immigrant farmers as part of broader initiatives developed for Latino/a entrepreneurs. For example, scholar-activist Alfonso Morales is bringing the stories and struggles of Latino/a farmers to the attention of the Latino/a groups associated with the American Bar Association and business school communities.[2] Whether in the halls of government institutions such as the USDA or the broader world of Latino/a civil rights work, activists and institutional employees are stepping forward to make immigrant voices in agriculture heard.

Crucial to all these organizations are the staff members who have created long-standing relationships in immigrant communities in their respective regions, building the trust that allows immigrant workers to feel safe and supported entering their doors. At a minimum, Spanish-speaking staff members are necessary for these connections to be made, and ideally staff who also have the cultural experience and competency to do the required outreach. At best, when staff are already part of the communities that need outreach, such as in the case of the Latino/a USDA staff in Washington State, the most lasting and deep connections are made possible. In cases where funding is not available to hire bilingual and culturally competent staff in the short term, employees must all be trained so there is consistency in how immigrants and other farmers of color are treated, and staff are aware of available resources and other institutions to refer them to.

Making structural institutional change is a long-term process. While technical fixes will not address the root causes of farmer inequality, there are some practical solutions that I saw utilized by practitioners and farmers that are already making a difference for farmers on a daily basis. Creating broadly available resources in Spanish and other languages, including technical materials such as Good Agricultural Practices certification and other national-level regulations, sales requirements for markets, and specific pictorial glossaries on pests and other farm-specific language, such as those created by the Crossroads Community Food Network, are crucial tools for immigrant farmers, for whom technical language skills are difficult to acquire. Moreover, sharing resources and trainings across counties and states, whether within government or nonprofit institutions, is a way to make these advances go further and create support for institutions to deepen such work.

There also must be policy changes at the state and national levels in order for organizational cultures to shift in a lasting and comprehensive manner. A good example of comprehensive state policy is the "Farmer Equity Act," AB 1348, which was signed into law by California governor Jerry Brown in 2017. This act specifically targets the California Department of Food and Agriculture to better provide resources, outreach, technical assistance, and decision-making power to "socially disadvantaged farmers and ranchers." In enacting the law, its authors stated it was created directly in response to historic racial discrimination against farmers of color. Going beyond the USDA's model of specific grants and programs for socially disadvantaged farmers, the act includes new parameters for how the California Department of Food and Agriculture creates regulations, forms governance committees, and manages funding programs (Pesticide Action Network 2017).

Further, we must find ways to incentivize and subsidize the passing of land and agricultural resources from farm owners to farmworkers. As I have discussed, there is a growing number of US-born farmers retiring from agriculture without children interested taking over the family farm. Many of these farmers would like to see their land stay in production and their rural towns remain vibrant and centered around feeding their communities rather than have their farmland developed into housing subdivisions or bought out by massive farming operations. Yet the very people who are knowledgeable and trained in operating these farms are priced out of buying the land and taking over the farm business. While there are nonprofit groups that are working to connect farmworkers and other immigrants and people of color with land, such as California FarmLink, mentioned in chapter 3, such organizations cannot support this transition on a large scale without more comprehensive government-based support. Making this land and resource transfer possible would benefit rural livelihoods and economies as well as consumer health and ecological sustainability. This shift should be a goal of all state- and national-level agricultural and health-focused institutions, from the USDA to the EPA.

Finally, and perhaps most challenging, we must advocate for a structural shift in who controls and profits from agricultural production, one that would make it possible for farmers to make ends meet without exploiting workers. While advocating for a living wage for farmworkers and strengthening agricultural labor regulations are crucial tasks given our current system, the reality is that most small-scale farmers can barely afford to pay themselves. Immigrant farmers certainly fall in the category of agrarian self-exploitation, and increased regulation alone will not help them raise labor standards for those whom they employ. The challenge that lies ahead includes ensuring that alternative and racially diverse farmers have better access to the market share, and that both farmers and workers benefit from producing more ecologically and socially just food.

Of course, it is impossible to discuss policy and institutional change without addressing the political moment in which we sit. While I write this conclusion, the president of the United States has condoned jailing immigrant children and separating them from their parents, and called for a national emergency to build a larger physical border between the United States and Mexico. It seems from the start of this research to the present, the situation for immigrants in the United States has only gone from bad to worse. But the people I met while conducting this study and the stories I have tried to relay in this book still give me hope. Immigrant workers and farmers are the heart, soul, and backbone of our current agrarian communities and economies in this country. They will persist and thrive as long as we all continue to eat. I can only hope that through this research and writing, I have added to the political case for their civil and human rights, and much-deserved respect, as essential members of our diverse, conflicted US society.

A Sustainable Future for Latino/a Immigrant Growers?

In this book, I have proposed new agrarian questions as well as some answers regarding race, migration, and citizenship. I have asked how racial and cultural politics matter in the construction of new agricultural transitions and shifting developments in access to land and capital, farming techniques, markets, and labor. This study exemplifies the ways that our understandings of agrarian change and possibilities for a more socially just and racially equitable food system rest in deconstructing the limitations as well as opportunities for farmers of color, immigrants, and others who have experienced historical and present-day discrimination in food and farming sectors. Only by looking closely at the differences in lived experiences between racialized groups of food producers, and appreciating both their race- and citizenship-based obstacles as well as unique offerings and skills, can we begin to form a new theory of agrarian change.

Immigrant farmers endeavor to use their agrarian experience and knowledge to escape their position as agricultural laborers and reclaim food production on their own terms, challenging an undemocratic and historically racist food system. They struggle to succeed in a food system where their racial positioning, as it intersects with their economic standing, makes their chances of owning a farm limited. These farmers, who do not fit the historical imagery of a successful family farmer in the United States are creating openings for nontraditional farmers, including those of color. By making brown-skinned farmers visible at farmers markets, in USDA offices, and other agricultural venues, they are normalizing the face of the nonwhite farmers, often in politically conservative regions of the country.

Despite their successes, they are competing in highly industrial global markets, which pressure them to reduce crop diversity, more frequently hire nonfamily labor, and more often sell to brokers and wholesalers versus direct markets. For some, this pressure is challenging the cultural values and lifestyle goals that inspired them to pursue farming in the United States in the first place. Remaining family operated and continuing to produce diverse crops will depend on their ability to find more direct and regional markets, and new ways to creatively sell their produce. The feat of starting a small family-run farm in the United States as immigrants and former farmworkers, struggling to avoid large-scale monocropped agriculture, both defies the odds of farming in a US system that discriminates against nonwhite farmers and exemplifies the challenges of creating a democratic, sustainable future for food.

For the time being, they are doing everything in their power to resist this pressure and relying on what limited resources they have to maintain these practices against the odds. Immigrant farmers in the United States do not fit the mold formed by current discussion on the agrarian question and agrarian class dynamics in that they are neither acquiescing to industrial agriculture nor consciously identifying with alternative food and agriculture movements. Their resilience points to the need for agrarian researchers and activists to consider transnational people as well as transnational politics, if a global agrarian movement is to coalesce and shift power dynamics in global agriculture. This research highlights the timeliness and importance of scholars and policy makers better incorporating issues of race, migration, and citizenship into their understandings of agricultural production and shifting class dynamics.

To create a more racially diverse agricultural system in the United States, there is work to be done. This book asks practitioners, researchers, and those who work in the world of alternative farming in particular to better recognize the persistence of nonwhite farmers in order build on our understanding of agricultural transitions and racial formations. Using the lenses of racial identity, immigration, and legibility, I have investigated how immigrant farmers are commonly excluded from state-supported opportunities, further marginalizing them from agricultural success and stability. The state and civil society are by no means separate entities, and many within the USDA and nonprofit organizations are actively working on creating reforms with regard to their history of racism. Yet until these institutional norms are challenged, many farmers of color, and immigrant farmers in particular, will continue to struggle to achieve agrarian class mobility, while landownership and food-producing industries will remain in primarily white hands.

The growing presence of nonwhite immigrant farmers and other farmers of color forces us to question whether farming must and will always reaffirm historical race and citizenship relations. As these farmers' stories remind us, agriculture and foodways across the United States' borders are wrought with stories of struggle and suffering, but they are also full of success and survival.

Farming is not an easy way to earn a living, especially when you have not inherited a family farm, have little capital input, and do not have the advantages of being born in the United States, and being part of the white majority of farm owners and operators. For Mexican immigrants who are converting from farmworker to farm owner, the explanation for their persistence in the profession must be analyzed beyond simple class mobility. Their growing presence in small-scale farming in the United States must be understood as one connected to agrarian culture and identity as they create a sense of place defined by their own experience.

It is this desire for an agrarian life and livelihood, not just a means of income, that inspires their drive to farm against the grain of industrial agriculture. The question as to what role they will play in the future of alternative agriculture in the United States remains. As immigrant farmers contest broadly conceived notions of farmers in the United States, they continue to face challenges to their economic and cultural survival as small-scale family farmers. It is only through fighting for and actively supporting a substantial structural, cultural, and institutional shift, in which immigrants and other farmers of color are embraced as essential contributors of agricultural knowledge, that we will see a sustainable future for everyone engaged in agriculture today.

Notes

Chapter 1

1. While there are no statistics showing the exact percentage of food products in the United States that are imported, evidence from US food processors, brokers, and wholesalers shows that many food products grown in the United States are being purchased from abroad (Oberholtzer, Dimitri, and Jaenicke 2013). Additionally, research conducted by the USDA's Economic Research Service (ERS) show that organic imports to the United States are currently higher than US exports in organic—$1.65 billion in imports versus $548 million in exports in 2016 (USDA-ERS 2018).

2. I did not use a sales minimum as an inclusion criterion, but I did require that participants were selling at least some of their crops for profit. The National Agricultural Statistics Service defines a farm as any business "from which $1,000 or more of agricultural products were sold or would normally be sold during the year" (USDA 2014). Beginning farmers of all backgrounds and ethnicities struggle to make ends meet, and few succeed at farming without supplemental off-farm income. Ninety-one percent of all US farming households have at least one person contributing from a nonfarm income (Brown and Weber 2013).

3. I also interviewed one farmer from El Salvador, one from Guatemala, and one from Honduras. Participants identified as Latino/a and/or Hispanic. I chose to use the term "Latino/a" as it is more inclusive of indigenous Mexican heritage. Although I am in agreement with and supportive of the transition to using the gender-inclusive "Latinx," I use "Latino/a" since that was the term most often used by participants in identifying themselves.

4. Indigenous Mexicans are the newest and fastest-growing group of farmworkers to California. They enter in the lowest-paying jobs in the agricultural labor market, and often struggle with social isolation from other immigrant farmworkers due to their different culture and language (Mines, Nichols, and Runsten 2010; Minkoff-Zern 2012).

5. According to the USDA-ERS (2017) glossary, "The farm operator is the person who runs the farm, making the day-to-day management decisions. The operator could be an owner, hired manager, cash tenant, share tenant, and/or a partner. If land is rented or worked on shares, the tenant or renter is the operator. In the recent Census of Agriculture and in the Agricultural Resource Management Survey (ARMS), information is collected for up to three operators per farm. In the case of multiple operators, the respondent for the farm identifies who the principal farm operator is during the data collection process."

6. This number is out of 2,109,303 total principal operators in 2012 (USDA 2014). The number of Hispanic/Latino operators who were also owners before 2012 is not available. These numbers do not tell us how many are first-generation immigrants.

7. This is with the exception of the work of Miriam Wells (1996), whose ground-breaking research in the 1970s and 1980s shed light on the class- and race-based struggles of Mexican and Japanese immigrants in California agriculture. More recently, a few other scholars have published work addressing the situation of Latino/a and immigrant farmers, including Adam Calo (2018) and Alfonso Morales (2011).

8. I have supplemented this qualitative study with quantitative analysis of the US Census of Agriculture on a state-by-state level with colleagues in a forthcoming manuscript, which I suggest reading in conjunction with this book (see Minkoff-Zern, Welsh, and Ludden, forthcoming).

9. It is possible to make initial economic gains from a small fruit and vegetable farm with less acreage and capital investment in equipment than some other types of agricultural production, such as grain or dairy, which require more expensive machinery as well as larger areas of land in order to be profitable in today's economy.

10. Half of the funding for ALBA comes from federal funding, including the USDA's Beginning Farmer and Rancher Development Program and the Socially Disadvantaged Farmers and Ranchers Program. The other half comes from the private sector, including about ten different foundations.

11. For further discussion of this group of farmers, see Guthman 2017.

12. This is with the exception of those farmers whose photographs are featured. I contacted them during the book publishing process to confirm that they still wished to have their names and identities shared publicly.

Chapter 2

1. In the traditional agricultural ladder metaphor, family labor, particularly that of the farmer's wife, is assumed. Without the additional labor of one's wife and children, a tenant or sharecropper had less chance of accessing land to rent, as a single man was not considered capable of running a farm himself (Foley 1999).

2. Confederate lands were returned to their pardoned prewar owners, following President Andrew Johnson's 1865 amnesty proclamation.

3. Lee Alston and Kyle Kauffman's (1998) historical analysis shows a similar number of black and white tenant farmers moving down the rungs of the agricultural ladder, or out of agriculture completely, during the 1910–1940 period. This study, though, demonstrates that more black farmers started at lower levels, as sharecroppers or tenant farmers, than white farmers did to begin with.

4. For more discussion of racial discrimination by the USDA, see *chapter 4.*

5. This agency has since been renamed as Immigration and Customs Enforcement or ICE.

6. In 2017, a new bill (H.R. 4092) was proposed in Congress to transfer control over the current guest worker program from the Department of Labor, where it currently resides, to the Department of Agriculture, where the farm lobby would have more direct control over the program. Additionally, the proposal included allowing farms to apply for year-round workers, not just seasonal ones. Although this bill ultimately failed, there have been continued efforts by the agricultural lobby to make the program accessible to a broader group of farmers and less regulated in terms of housing requirements and oversight.

7. This is based on the most recently available data. The last agricultural census was conducted in 2017, but results were not publicly available at the time of this book's printing.

8. See Ostrom 2005; Ostrom and Jackson-Smith 2005; Ostrom, Cha, and Flores 2010.

Chapter 3

1. I am not claiming that Washington is the only state with Spanish-speaking USDA staff, only that this is the one state in my study where I was able to access them for interviews.

2. As I discuss in the conclusion of this chapter, there are currently efforts to increase the number of extension staff who do outreach to Latino/a farmers in Virginia.

3. This can be true for beginning white farmers, who are also excluded from new markets, especially in major metropolises like the San Francisco Bay Area, where local markets for alternatively produced fruits and vegetables are saturated. Yet as this research shows, for farmers of color, the barriers to enter agrarian spaces where they are not merely laborers are especially high.

4. The claims process was conducted by an outside contractor, as is confirmed in the USDA's Inspector General Audit Report (Harden 2016).

5. Of the immigrant orchardists I interviewed (mostly monocrop producers), all had gone through the FSA program for loans to purchase land and equipment, but as I discuss in *chapter 4*, in many ways they were not the norm among the farmers I interviewed.

6. Lacking a business plan has been specifically cited as a limitation for Latino/a farmers in other regions and studies as well (Martinez-Feria 2011; Starkweather et al. 2011).

7. For more information, see https://attra.ncat.org/about-us/.

8. I last checked these websites on February 21, 2018.

9. While I cannot be certain that the decrease in Spanish language documents on the USDA website is in direct correlation to the Trump administration, the fact that the administration actively deactivated the Spanish version of the White House webpage, scrubbed key terms such as "climate change" from the EPA and National Park Services sites, and removed references to LGBTQ persons from the state department site makes these disappearances seem suspicious as to their timing.

10. This experience is reflective of the treatment of enslaved and freed African Americans who attempted to make a living through food sales in the antebellum US South (Harris 2011; Williams-Forson 2006).

11. This is certainly true among farmworkers as well, as is evidenced in Teresa Mares's work on undocumented workers, fear, and mobility near the northern US border (Mares, Wolcott-MacCausland, Mazar 2017; Mares 2019).

Chapter 4

1. They were geographic outliers in my research, located 10 miles from Ithaca, New York, and 250 miles northwest of New York City. A good friend, who is a white organic farmer, knows them through local networks of small farmers in the region and introduced me when I told her about my research.

2. Since this interview was conducted, Carlos and Lorena have closed their farming business due to financial straits and the stress of a growing family. They are still active in the agricultural community and have plans to restart their business once they are more financially secure.

3. Although in this book I focus on low-input and organic practices utilized by immigrants with farming backgrounds from Mexico, and most of them stated that this reflects their farming approaches previous to migration, not all small-scale subsistence farmers in Mexico and the surrounding region use strictly low-input techniques. Many small-scale farmers in Mexico and Latin America more generally practice chemically intensive agriculture (Galt 2008).

4. There are white farmers in all these regions involved in growing diverse crops and using alternative growing practices more broadly. In my research, I found immigrant farmers were engaging these practices more regularly than white farmers. As I discuss in *chapter 2*, census data confirms my findings.

5. For more discussion of the agricultural census, see *chapter 2*.

6. She is implying that although the farmers may have paperwork stating they are in the United States legally, this paperwork might be falsified.

7. For a more in-depth discussion of undocumented workers, see *chapter 2*.

Chapter 5

1. As I discuss later in the chapter, family labor does not ensure more just conditions by default.

2. These tensions and contradictions regarding the relationship between peasant farmers and capitalist agrarian development have been debated by scholars engaging with the so-called agrarian question. The agrarian question debate stems from Karl Marx's discussion of the peasants' role in class transition to capitalism, and has been perpetuated by scholars striving to understand these transitions in particular historical moments (see, among others, Marx 2008; Lenin 1972; Kautsky 1988; Chayanov 1986). In more recent iterations, literature on repeasantization has drawn on these debates, arguing that the relevance of discussing agrarian transition has been revived by the actions of today's small-scale farmers across the globe as they reclaim land and foodways to promote more localized systems of food production as well as consumption (see, among others, Akram-Lohdi 2013; Goodman and Watts 1997; McMichael 2013; van der Ploeg 2013).

3. Agroecological farming being a more specific subset of what I identify as alternative farming practices.

4. In a study for the Mexican government, the World Bank found that the extreme rural poverty rate was 35 percent in 1992–1994, before NAFTA was enacted. The rate jumped to 55 percent in 1996–1998, after NAFTA took effect. Following this increase in rural poverty, the number of Mexicans living in the United States doubled in the years 1990 to 2000, as people displaced from farming migrated to the United States seeking employment (Bacon 2012).

5. Although some Spaniards went through legal channels to purchase land from native owners, landownership arrangements were often redrawn to consolidate land, while pushing indigenous populations onto smaller shared parcels and into concentrated villages.

6. In response to NAFTA and the cancellation of Article 27, self-identified indigenous peasant farmers rebelled in the southern state of Chiapas. The Zapatista Army

of National Liberation declared war on the Mexican state the day NAFTA was signed. Although the official uprising only lasted twelve days, it was the public declaration of a social movement and force of resistance against the neoliberal reforms of NAFTA and land reconcentration. The Zapatistas have locally instated many of their own land reforms based on the ejido system in an effort to reappropriate land to native peasant farmers (Harvey 1996; Stephen 1997).

7. They are fortunate among farmworkers, as wage theft and daily hiring is common in the agriculture industry (Fox et al. 2017).

8. For more on racialized labor hierarchies in US agriculture, see Holmes 2013.

9. The state minimum wage in New York was $8.75 at the time of this interview. Antonio is implying he was being paid $3.60 below the minimum wage.

Chapter 6

1. See http://www.soulfirefarm.org/; Nedra Rhone, "Black Farmers in Georgia Reclaiming Agricultural Roots," *Talk of the Town Blog*, August 29, 2018, https://www .ajc.com/blog/talk-town/black-farmers-georgia-reclaiming-agricultural-roots/ WM20O5kYme6c7MtsCjgSnL/

2. See https://futureoflatinos.org/co-directors/.

References

Abarca, Meredith E. 2006. *Voices in the Kitchen: Views of Food and the World from Working-Class Mexican and Mexican American Women.* College Station: Texas A&M University Press.

Abarca, Meredith E. 2017. "Afro-Latina/os' Culinary Subjectivities: Rooting Ethnicities through Root Vegetables." In *Food across Borders,* edited by Matt Garcia, E. Melanie DuPuis, and Don Mitchell, 24–43. New Brunswick, NJ: Rutgers University Press.

Ahearn, Mary Clare, Jet Yee, and Penni Korb. 2005. "Effects of Differing Farm Policies on Farm Structure and Dynamics." *American Journal of Agricultural Economics* 87, no. 5 (December): 1182–1189.

Akram-Lodhi, A. Haroon. 2013. *Hungry for Change: Farmers, Food Justice and the Agrarian Question.* Sterling, VA: Kumarian Press Inc.

Alkon, Alison Hope. 2007. "Growing Resistance: Food, Culture and the Mo' Better Foods Farmers' Market." *Gastronomica* 7, no. 3 (Summer): 93–99.

Alkon, Alison Hope. 2008. "From Value to Values: Sustainable Consumption at Farmers Markets." *Agriculture and Human Values* 25, no. 4 (December): 487–498.

Alkon, Alison Hope. 2012. *Black, White, and Green: Farmers Markets, Race, and the Green Economy.* Vol. 13. Athens: University of Georgia Press.

Alkon, Alison Hope, and Julian Agyeman. 2011. *Cultivating Food Justice: Race, Class, and Sustainability.* Cambridge, MA: MIT Press

Alkon, Alison Hope, and Christie Grace McCullen. 2011. "Whiteness and Farmers Markets: Performances, Perpetuations ... Contestations?" *Antipode* 43, no. 4 (September): 937–959.

Allen, Patricia. 2004. *Together at the Table: Sustainability and Sustenance in the American Agrifood System.* University Park: Penn State University Press, 2004.

Allen, Patricia. 2008. "Mining for Justice in the Food System: Perceptions, Practices, and Possibilities." *Agriculture and Human Values* 25, no. 2 (June): 157–161.

Allen, Patricia, Margaret FitzSimmons, Michael Goodman, and Keith Warner. 2003. "Shifting Plates in the Agrifood Landscape: The Tectonics of Alternative Agrifood Initiatives in California." *Journal of Rural Studies* 19, no. 1 (January): 61–75.

Alonso-Fradejas, Alberto, Saturnino M. Borras Jr., Todd Holmes, Eric Holt-Giménez, and Martha Jane Robbins. 2015. "Food Sovereignty: Convergence and Contradictions, Conditions and Challenges." *Third World Quarterly* 36, no. 3 (March): 431–448.

Alston, Lee J., and Kyle D. Kauffman. 1998. "Up, Down, and Off the Agricultural Ladder: New Evidence and Implications of Agricultural Mobility for Blacks in the Postbellum South." *Agricultural History* 72, no. 2 (April): 263–279.

Altman, Ida, Sarah L. Cline, and Juan Javier Pescador. 2003. *The Early History of Greater Mexico*. Upper Saddle River, NJ: Prentice Hall.

Assies, Willem. 2008. "Land Tenure and Tenure Regimes in Mexico: An Overview." *Journal of Agrarian Change* 8, no. 1 (January): 33–63.

Bacon, David. 2012. "How U.S. Policies Fueled Mexico's Great Migration." *Nation*, January 23. https://www.thenation.com/article/how-us-policies-fueled-mexicos-great-migration/.

Barham, Elizabeth. 1997. "Social Movements for Sustainable Agriculture in France: A Polanyian Perspective." *Society and Natural Resources* 10, no. 3 (May): 239–249.

Barndt, Deborah. 2008. *Tangled Routes: Women, Work, and Globalization on the Tomato Trail*. Lanham, MD: Rowman and Littlefield Publishers.

Borah, Woodrow W. 1983. *Justice by Insurance: The General Indian Court of Colonial Mexico and the Legal Aides of the Half-Real*. Berkeley: University of California Press.

Bowens, Natasha. 2015a. "The Color of Food: America's Invisible Farmers." *Civil Eats*, April 14. Accessed June 19, 2018. https://civileats.com/2015/04/14/the-color-of-food-an-introduction/.

Bowens, Natasha. 2015b. *The Color of Food: Stories of Race, Resilience and Farming*. Gabriola Island, BC: New Society Publishers.

Brading, David A. 1991. *The First America: The Spanish Monarchy, Creole Patriots and the Liberal State, 1492–1867*. Cambridge: Cambridge University Press.

Brent, Zoe W., Christina M. Schiavoni, and Alberto Alonso-Fradejas. 2015. "Contextualising Food Sovereignty: The Politics of Convergence among Movements in the USA." *Third World Quarterly* 36, no. 3 (April): 618–635.

Brown, Jason P., and Jeremy G. Weber. 2013. "The Off-Farm Occupations of U.S. Farm Operators and Their Spouses." *USDA-ERS Economic Information Bulletin* 117 (September). Accessed January 24, 2019. https://ssrn.com/abstract=2323640.

Brown, Sandy, and Christy Getz. 2008. "Privatizing Farm Worker Justice: Regulating Labor through Voluntary Certification and Labeling." *Geoforum* 39 (3): 1184–1196.

Buck, Pem Davidson. 2001. *Worked to the Bone: Race, Class, Power, and Privilege in Kentucky.* New York: Monthly Review Press.

Buttel, Frederick H., and William L. Flinn. 1975. "Sources of Consequences of Agrarian Values in American Society." *Rural Sociology* 40, no. 2 (Summer): 134–151.

California Strawberry Commission. 2014. *Growing the American Dream: California Strawberry Farming's Rich History of Immigrants and Opportunity.* Watsonville: California Strawberry Commission. Accessed July 31, 2017. http://www.calstrawberry .com/Portals/0/Reports/Community%20Reports/Growing%20the%20American%20 Dream.pdf.

Calo, Adam. 2018. "How Knowledge Deficit Interventions Fail to Resolve Beginning Farmer Challenges." *Agriculture and Human Values* 35, no. 2 (June): 367–381.

Chan, Sucheng. 1989. *This Bittersweet Soil: The Chinese in California Agriculture, 1860– 1910.* Berkeley: University of California Press.

Clapp, Jennifer. 2012. *Food.* Cambridge, UK: Polity Press.

Chayanov, A. V. 1986. *AV Chayanov on the Theory of Peasant Economy.* Edited by D. Thorner, B. H. Kerblay, and R. E. F. Smith. Manchester: Manchester University Press. First published 1919.

Clemens, Michael. 2013. "The Effect of Foreign Labor on Native Employment: A Job-Specific Approach and Application to North Carolina Farms." Working Paper 326. Washington, DC: Center for Global Development.

Cline, Sarah L. 1986. *Colonial Culhuacan, 1580–1600: A Social History of an Aztec Town.* Albuquerque: University of New Mexico Press.

Cohen, William. 1991. *At Freedom's Edge: Black Mobility and the Southern White Quest for Racial Control, 1861–1915.* Baton Rouge, LA: LSU Press.

Couto, Richard A. 1991. "Heroic Bureaucracies." *Administration and Society* 23, no. 1 (May): 123–147.

Cox, LaWanda. 1958. "The Promise of Land for the Freedmen." *Mississippi Valley Historical Review* 45, no. 3 (December): 413–440.

Daniel, Pete. 2013. *Dispossession: Discrimination against African American Farmers in the Age of Civil Rights.* Chapel Hill: University of North Carolina Press.

Dimitri, Carolyn, Anne Effland, and Nelson Conklin. 2005. *The 20th Century Transformation of U.S. Agriculture and Farm Policy.* Economic Information Bulletin No. 3. Washington, DC: US Department of Agriculture, Economic Research Service.

DuPuis, E. Melanie. 2002. *Nature's Perfect Food: How Milk Became America's Drink.* New York: NYU Press.

Eisenstadt, Todd A. 2009. "Agrarian Tenure Institution, Conflict Frames, and Communitarian Identities: The Case of Indigenous Southern Mexico." *Comparative Political Studies* 42, no. 1 (January): 82–113.

Feldman, Shelley, and Rick Welsh. 1995. "Feminist Knowledge Claims, Local Knowledge, and Gender Divisions of Agricultural Labor: Constructing a Successor Science." *Rural Sociology* 60, no. 1 (April): 23–43.

Flynn, Charles L., Jr. 1999. *White Land, Black Labor: Caste and Class in Late Nineteenth-Century Georgia.* Baton Rouge, LA: LSU Press.

Foley, Neal. 1999. *The White Scourge: Mexicans, Blacks, and Poor Whites in Texas Cotton Culture.* Berkeley: University of California Press.

Fox, Carly, Rebecca Fuentes, Fabiola Ortiz Valdez, Gretchen Purser, and Kathleen Sexsmith. 2017. *MILKED: Immigrant Dairy Farmworkers in New York State.* Workers' Center of Central New York and Worker Justice Center of New York.

Galt, Ryan E. 2008. "Toward an Integrated Understanding of Pesticide Use Intensity in Costa Rican Vegetable Farming." *Human Ecology* 36, no. 5 (October): 655–677.

Garcia, Matt. 2002. *A World of Its Own: Race, Labor, and Citrus in the Making of Greater Los Angeles, 1900–1970.* Chapel Hill: University of North Carolina Press.

Gilbert, Jess. 2015. *Planning Democracy: Agrarian Intellectuals and the Intended New Deal.* New Haven, CT: Yale University Press.

Gilbert, Jess, Gwen Sharp, and M. Sindy Felin. 2002. "The Loss and Persistence of Black-Owned Farmland: A Review of the Research Literature and Its Implications." *Southern Rural Sociology* 18 (2): 1–30.

Goodman, David, E. Melanie DuPuis, and Michael K. Goodman. 2012. *Alternative Food Networks: Knowledge, Practice, and Politics.* New York: Routledge.

Goodman, David, and Michael Redclift. 1985. "Capitalism, Petty Commodity Production, and the Farm Enterprise." *Sociologia Ruralis* 25, nos. 3–4 (December): 231–247.

Goodman, David, and Michael J. Watts, eds. 1997. *Globalising Food: Agrarian Questions and Global Restructuring.* New York: Routledge.

Gray, Margaret. 2013. *Labor and the Locavore: The Making of a Comprehensive Food Ethic.* Berkeley: University of California Press.

Grim, Valerie. 1996. "Black Participation in the Farmers Home Administration and Agricultural Stabilization and Conservation Service, 1964–1990." *Agricultural History* 70, no. 2 (April): 321–336.

Guthman, Julie. 2008a. "Bringing Good Food to Others: Investigating the Subjects of Alternative Agrifood Practices." *Cultural Geographies* 15, no. 4 (October): 431–447.

Guthman, Julie. 2008b. "If They Only Knew: Colorblindness and Universalism in Alternative Agrifood Institutions." *Professional Geographer* 60, no. 3 (August): 387–397.

Guthman, Julie. 2014. *Agrarian Dreams: The Paradox of Organic Farming in California.* Berkeley: University of California Press.

Guthman, Julie. 2017. "Life Itself Under Contract: Rent-Seeking and Biopolitical Devolution through Partnerships in California's Strawberry Industry." *Journal of Peasant Studies* 44, no. 1 (January): 100–117.

Guthman, Julie, and Sandy Brown. 2016. "I Will Never Eat Another Strawberry Again: The Biopolitics of Consumer-Citizenship in the Fight against Methyl Iodide in California." *Agriculture and Human Values* 33, no. 3 (September): 575–585.

Hahamovitch, Cindy. 1997. *The Fruits of Their Labor: Atlantic East Coast Farmworkers and the Making of Migrant Poverty, 1870–1945.* Chapel Hill: University of North Carolina Press.

Hall, Stuart. 1990. "Cultural Identity and Diaspora." In *Identity: Community, Culture, Difference*, edited by Jonathan Rutherford, 222–237. London: Lawrence and Wishart.

Harden, Gil. H. 2016. *Hispanic and Women Farmers and Ranchers Claim Resolution Process.* Audit Report No. 50601-0002-21. US Department of Agriculture, Office of Inspector General, Washington, DC. Accessed February 3, 2019. https://www.usda.gov/oig/webdocs/50601-0002-21.pdf.

Harper, Breeze A. 2010. *Sistah Vegan: Black Female Vegans Speak on Food, Identity, Health, and Society.* Brooklyn: Lantern Books.

Harris, Jessica B. 2011. *High on the Hog: A Culinary Journey from Africa to America.* New York: Bloomsbury Publishing.

Harrison, Jill Lindsey. 2011. *Pesticide Drift and the Pursuit of Environmental Justice.* Cambridge, MA: MIT Press.

Harvey, Neil. 1996. "Rural Reforms and the Zapatista Rebellion: Chiapas, 1998–1995." In *Neoliberalism Revisited: Economic Restructuring and Mexico's Political Future*, edited by Gerardo Otero, 187–208. New York: Routledge.

Harvey, Robert. 2000. *Liberators: Latin America's Struggle for Independence.* Woodstock, NY: Overlook Press.

Henderson, George. 1998. "Nature and Fictitious Capital: The Historical Geography of an Agrarian Question." *Antipode* 30, no. 2 (April): 73–118.

Hispanic and Women Farmers and Ranchers Claims and Resolution Process. 2012. Accessed June 4, 2018. https://www.usda.gov/oig/webdocs/50601-0002-21.pdf.

Holmes, Seth. 2013. *Fresh Fruit, Broken Bodies: Migrant Farmworkers in the United States*. Berkeley: University of California Press.

Hornick, Mike. 2015. "Strawberry Commission Taps First Latina Chair." *Packer*. Accessed July 31, 2017. http://www.thepacker.com/news/strawberry-commission -taps-first-latina-chair.

Kasarda, John D., and James H. Johnson Jr. 2006. *The Economic Impact of the Hispanic Population on the State of North Carolina*. Chapel Hill, NC: Frank Hawkins Kenan Institute of Private Enterprise.

Kautsky, Karl. 1988. *The Agrarian Question*. Translated by Pete Burgess. London: Zwan Publications. First published 1899.

Keen, Benjamin, and Keith Haynes. 2012. *A History of Latin America*. Boston: Cengage Learning.

Kloppenburg, Jack R. 2005. *First the Seed: The Political Economy of Plant Biotechnology*. Madison: University of Wisconsin Press.

Kloppenburg, Jack R., and Charles C. Geisler. 1985. "The Agricultural Ladder: Agrarian Ideology and the Changing Structure of U.S. Agriculture." *Journal of Rural Studies* 1 (1): 59–72.

Koohafkan, Parviz, and Miguel A. Altieri. 2016. *Forgotten Agricultural Heritage: Reconnecting Food Systems and Sustainable Development*. New York: Routledge.

La Via Campesina. 2018. Member Organisations of La Via Campesina. Accessed February 6, 2019. https://viacampesina.org/en/member-organisations-of-la-via-cam pesina-updated-2018/.

Lee, Chana Kai. 2000. *For Freedom's Sake: The Life of Fannie Lou Hamer*. Champaign: University of Illinois Press.

Lee, Shu-Ching. 1947. "The Theory of the Agricultural Ladder." *Agricultural History* 21, no. 1 (January): 53–61.

Lenin, Vladimir Il'ich. 1972. *The Development of Capitalism in Russia*. Moscow: Progress Publishers. First published 1899.

Lockhart, James. 1969. "Encomienda and Hacienda: The Evolution of the Great Estate in the Spanish Indies." *Hispanic American Historical Review* 49, no. 3 (August): 411–429.

Lucht, Jill R. 2006. *Latinos in Southwest Missouri: Capturing the American Dream through Farming*. Latinos in Missouri Occasional Paper Series, No. 5. Columbia: Department of Rural Sociology, University of Missouri. Accessed February 2, 2019. http://www.cambio.missouri.edu/Library/LatinosInMo/papers/Lucht.pdf.

Mann, Charles C. 2005. *1491: New Revelations o the Americas before Columbus*. New York: Knopf.

Mapes, Kathleen. 2004 "'A Special Class of Labor': Mexican (Im)migrants, Immigration Debate, and Industrial Agriculture in the Rural Midwest." *Labor: Studies in Working-Class History of the Americas* 1, no. 2 (June): 65–88.

Mares, Teresa M. 2012. "Tracing Immigrant Identity through the Plate and the Palate." *Latino Studies* 10, no. 3 (Fall): 334–354.

Mares, Teresa M. 2019. *Life on the Other Border: Farmworkers and Food Justice in Vermont*. Berkeley: University of California Press.

Mares, Teresa M., and Devon Gerardo Peña. 2010. "Urban Agriculture in the Making of Insurgent Spaces in Los Angeles and Seattle." In *Insurgent Public Space: Guerrilla Urbanism and the Remaking of the Contemporary City*, edited by Jeffrey Hou, 241–254. New York: Routledge.

Mares, Teresa M., Naomi Wolcott-MacCausland, and Jessie Mazar. 2017. "Eating Far from Home: Latino/a Workers and Food Sovereignty in Rural Vermont." In *Food across Borders*, edited by Matt Garcia, E. Melanie DuPuis, and Don Mitchell, 181–200. New Brunswick, NJ: Rutgers University Press.

Martin, Philip. 2003. *Economic Integration and Migration: The Mexico-US Case*. Discussion Paper 2003/35. Helsinki: UN University World Institute for Development Economics Research.

Martinez, Juan, and R. Edmund Gomez. 2011. *Identifying Barriers That Prevent Hispanic/Latino Farmers and Ranchers in Washington State from Participating in USDA Programs and Services*. Yakima, WA: Rural Community Development Resources Center for Latino Farmers.

Martinez-Feria, Rafael. 2011. *Barriers, Challenges and Limitations That Hispanic and Latino Farmers and Ranchers Face to Start, Develop and Sustain Farming and Ranching Businesses in the State of Nebraska*. Lyons, NE: Center for Rural Affairs. Accessed February 2, 2019. http://files.cfra.org/pdf/barriers-hispanic-latino-farmer-rancher-report.pdf.

Massey, Doreen B. 1994. *Space, Place, and Gender*. Minneapolis: University of Minnesota Press.

Matsumoto, Valerie J. 1993. *Farming the Home Place: A Japanese American Community in California, 1919–1982*. Ithaca, NY: Cornell University Press.

Marx, Karl. 2008. *Capital*. Edited by David McLellan. Oxford: Oxford University Press. First published 1887.

McCutcheon, Priscilla. 2013. "'Returning Home to Our Rightful Place': The Nation of Islam and Muhammad Farms." *Geoforum* 49 (October): 61–70.

McKenzie, Robert Tracy. 1993. "Freedmen and the Soil in the Upper South: The Reorganization of Tennessee Agriculture, 1865–1880." *Journal of Southern History* 59, no. 1 (February): 63–84.

McMichael, Philip. 2013. *Food Regimes and Agrarian Questions*. Halifax: Fernwood Publishing.

Mines, Richard, Sandra Nichols, and David Runsten. 2010. *California's Indigenous Farmworkers*. Final Report of the Indigenous Farmworker Study to the California Endowment. Accessed April 4, 2019. http://www.indigenousfarmworkers.org/IFS%20Full%20Report%20_Jan2010.pdf.

Minkoff-Zern, Laura-Anne. 2012. "Pushing the Boundaries of Indigeneity and Agricultural Knowledge: Oaxacan Immigrant Gardening in California." *Agriculture and Human Values* 29, no. 3 (September): 381–392.

Minkoff-Zern, Laura-Anne. 2014a. "Challenging the Agrarian Imaginary: Farmworker-Led Food Movements and the Potential for Farm Labor Justice." *Human Geography* 7 (1): 85–101.

Minkoff-Zern, Laura-Anne. 2014b. "Hunger Amidst Plenty: Farmworker Food Insecurity and Coping Strategies in California." *Local Environment* 19, no. 2 (February): 204–219.

Minkoff-Zern, Laura-Anne. 2014c. "Knowing 'Good Food': Immigrant Knowledge and the Racial Politics of Farmworker Food Insecurity." *Antipode* 46, no. 5 (November): 1190–1204.

Minkoff-Zern, Laura-Anne, Nancy Peluso, Jennifer Sowerwine, and Christy Getz. 2011. "Race and Regulation: Asian Immigrants in California Agriculture." In *Cultivating Food Justice: Race, Class, and Sustainability*, edited by Alison Hope Alkon and Julian Agyeman, 65–85. Cambridge, MA: MIT Press.

Minkoff-Zern, Laura-Anne, Rick Welsh, and Maddy T. Ludden. Forthcoming. "Immigrant Farmers, Sustainable Practices: Growing Ecological and Racial Diversity in Alternative Agrifood Spaces."

Mitchell, Don. 1996. *The Lie of the Land: Migrant Workers and the California Landscape*. Minneapolis: University of Minnesota Press.

Mitchell, Don. 2012. *They Saved the Crops: Labor, Landscape, and the Struggle over Industrial Farming in Bracero-Era California*. Athens: University of Georgia Press.

Mize, Ronald L., and Alicia C. S. Swords. 2010. *Consuming Mexican Labor: From the Bracero Program to NAFTA*. Toronto: University of Toronto Press.

Morales, Alfonso. 2011. "Growing Food and Justice: Dismantling Racism through Sustainable Food Systems." In *Cultivating Food Justice: Race, Class, and Sustainability*, edited by Alison Hope Alkon and Julian Agyeman, 149–176. Cambridge, MA: MIT Press.

Nadal, Alejandro. 2002. *Corn in NAFTA: Eight Years After*. Report prepared for the North American Commission for Environmental Cooperation. Mexico City: Science and Technology Program, El Colegio de México.

National Sustainable Agriculture Coalition. 2018. "Racial Equity in the Farm Bill: Barriers for Farmers of Color." Accessed June 19, 2018. http://sustainableagriculture .net/blog/racial-equity-in-farm-bill-barriers/.

Nock, Magdalena Barros. 2000. "The Mexican Peasantry and the Ejido in the Neoliberal Period." In *Disappearing Peasantries? Rural Labour in Africa, Asia, and Latin America*, edited by Deborah Bryceson, Cristóbal Kay, and Jos Mooij, 159–175. London: Intermediate Technology Publications.

Oberholtzer, Lydia, Carolyn Dimitri, and Edward C. Jaenicke. 2013. "International Trade of Organic Food: Evidence of U.S. Imports." *Renewable Agriculture and Food Systems* 28, no. 3 (September): 255–262.

Omi, Michael, and Howard Winant. 2014. *Racial Formation in the United States*. New York: Routledge.

Ostrom, Marcia. 2005. *The Importance of Direct Markets for Washington Farmers*. Research Brief Series 2005-03-08. Puyallup, WA: Center for Sustaining Agriculture and Natural Resources, Washington State University.

Ostrom, Marcia, Bee Cha, and Malaquías Flores. 2010. "Creating Access to Land Grant Resources for Multicultural and Disadvantaged Farmers." *Journal of Agriculture, Food Systems, and Community Development* 1, no. 1 (August): 89–105.

Ostrom, Marcia, and Douglas Jackson-Smith. 2005. "Defining a Purpose: Diverse Farm Constituencies and Publicly Funded Agricultural Research and Extension." *Journal of Sustainable Agriculture* 27, no. 3 (March): 57–76.

Pandoongpatt, Tanachi Mark. 2017. "'Chasing the Yum': Food Procurement and Thai American Community Formation in an Era before Free Trade." In *Food across Borders*, edited by Matt Garcia, E. Melanie DuPuis, and Don Mitchell, 79–104. New Brunswick, NJ: Rutgers University Press.

Patel, Raj. 2009. "Food Sovereignty." *Journal of Peasant Studies* 36, no. 3 (July): 663–706.

Payne, William C., Jr. 1991. "Institutional Discrimination in Agriculture Programs." *Rural Sociologist* 11, no. 1 (Winter): 16–18.

Paynter, Kevon. 2018. "Black Farmers Reviving Their African Roots: 'We Are Feeding Our Liberation.'" *Civil Eats*, Accessed June 26, 2018. https://civileats.com/2018/04/05/black-farmers-reviving-their-african-roots-we-are-feeding-our-liberation/.

Peña, Devon Gerardo. 1999. "Los Animalitos: Culture, Ecology, and the Politics of Place in the Upper Rio Grande." In *Chicano Culture, Ecology, Politics: Subversive Kin*, edited by Devon Gerardo Peña. Tucson: University of Arizona Press.

Peña, Devon Gerardo. 2005. *Mexican Americans and the Environment: Tierra y Vida*. Tucson: University of Arizona Press.

Penniman, Leah. 2017. "4 Not-So-Easy Ways to Dismantle Racism in the Food System." *YES! Magazine*. Accessed June 26, 2018. http://www.yesmagazine.org/people-power/4-not-so-easy-ways-to-dismantle-racism-in-the-food-system-20170427.

Pesticide Action Network. 2017. "Farmer Equity Act Recognizes Racial Discrimination, Enables State to Identify Barriers and Provide Much-Needed Support to Farmers." Accessed June 5, 2018. http://www.panna.org/press-release/farmer-equity-act.

Pilcher, Jeffrey M. 1996. "Tamales or Timbales: Cuisine and the Formation of Mexican National Identity, 1821–1911." *Americas* 53, no. 2 (October): 193–216.

Pilcher, Jeffrey M. 1998. *Que vivan los tamales!: Food and the Making of Mexican Identity*. Albuquerque: University of New Mexico Press.

Ponder, Henry. 1971. "Prospects for Black Farmers in the Years Ahead." *American Journal of Agricultural Economics* 53, no. 2 (May): 297–301.

Powell, Benjamin. 2012. "The Law of Unintended Consequences: Georgia's Immigration Law Backfires." *Forbes*, May 17. https://www.forbes.com/sites/realspin/2012/05/17/the-law-of-unintended-consequences-georgias-immigration-law-backfires/#61aac1b5492a.

Reed, Deborah B., Susan C. Westneat, Steven R. Browning, and Lana Skarke. 1999. "The Hidden Work of the Farm Homemaker." *Journal of Agricultural Safety and Health* 5 (3): 317–327.

Relinger, Rick. 2010. "NAFTA and U.S. Corn Subsidies: Explaining the Displacement of Mexico's Corn Farmers." *Prospect: Journal of International Affairs at UCSD* (April 19). Accessed February 6, 2019. https://prospectjournal.org/2010/04/19/nafta-and-u-s-corn-subsidies-explaining-the-displacement-of-mexicos-corn-farmers/comment-page-1/.

Reynolds, Kristin, and Nevin Cohen. 2016. *Beyond the Kale: Urban Agriculture and Social Justice Activism in New York City*. Athens: University of Georgia Press.

Riley, Mark. 2009. "Bringing the 'Invisible Farmer' into Sharper Focus: Gender Relations and Agricultural Practices in the Peak District (UK)." *Gender, Place and Culture* 16, no. 6 (December): 665–682.

Rovegno, Gabrielle. 2016. "Recommendations for Agricultural Service Agencies for Improving Programming Targeted for Hispanic/Latino Farmers." Master's thesis, Oklahoma State University.

Sbicca, Joshua. 2015. "Food Labor, Economic Inequality, and the Imperfect Politics of Process in the Alternative Food Movement." *Agriculture and Human Values* 32, no. 4 (December): 675–687.

Schweninger, Loren. 1989. "A Vanishing Breed: Black Farm Owners in the South, 1651–1982. *Agricultural History* 63, no. 3 (July): 41–60.

Scott, James C. 1998. *Seeing Like a State: How Certain Schemes to Improve the Human Condition Have Failed.* New Haven, CT: Yale University Press.

Sexsmith, Kathleen. 2017. "Milking Networks for All They're Worth: Precarious Migrant Life and the Process of Consent on New York Dairies." In *Food across Borders*, edited by Matt Garcia, E. Melanie DuPuis, and Don Mitchell, 201–218. New Brunswick, NJ: Rutgers University Press.

Shreck, Aime, Christy Getz, and Gail Feenstra. 2006. "Social Sustainability, Farm Labor, and Organic Agriculture: Findings from an Exploratory Analysis." *Agriculture and Human Values* 23, no. 4 (December): 439–449.

Simon, M. F. 1993. "Addressing the Problems of Agency Utilization by Kentucky's Black Limited Resource Farmers: Case Studies." In *Challenges in Agriculture and Rural Development: Proceedings of the 50th Annual Professional Agricultural Workers Conference*, edited by R. Zabawa, N. Baharanyi, and W. Hill, 129–134. Tuskegee, AL: Tuskegee University.

Slocum, Rachel. 2007. "Whiteness, Space, and Alternative Agrifood Practice." *Geoforum* 38, no. 3 (May): 520–533.

Slocum, Rachel. 2008. "Thinking Race through Corporeal Feminist Theory: Divisions and Intimacies at the Minneapolis Farmers' Market." *Social and Cultural Geography* 9, no. 8 (December): 849–869.

Slocum, Rachel, and Arun Saldanha. 2013. *Geographies of Race and Food: Fields, Bodies, Markets.* New York: Routledge.

Sowerwine, Jennifer, Christy Getz, and Nancy Peluso. 2015. "The Myth of the Protected Worker: Southeast Asian Micro-Farmers in California Agriculture." *Agriculture and Human Values* 32, no. 4 (December): 579–595.

Spillman, William J. 1919. "The Agricultural Ladder." *American Economic Review* 9, no. 1 (March): 170–179.

Starkweather, Kathie, Jon Bailey, Kim Preston, Stephen Jeanetta, and Eleazar U. Gonzalez. 2011. *Improving the Use of USDA Programs among Hispanic and Latino Farmers and Ranchers.* Lyons, NE: Center for Rural Affairs and Cambio Center. Accessed

February 2, 2019. http://files.cfra.org/pdf/improve-usda-program-use-hispanic-latino
-farmers.pdf.

Stephen, Lynn. 1997. "Pro-Zapatista and Pro-PRI: Resolving the Contradictions of
Zapatismo in Rural Oaxaca." *Latin American Research Review* 32, no. 2 (January):
41–70.

Stine, Linda France. 1990. "Social Inequality and Turn-of-the-Century Farmsteads:
Issues of Class, Status, Ethnicity, and Race." *Historical Archaeology* 24, no. 4 (January): 37–49.

Swisher, M. E., Mark Brennan, and Mital Shah. 2006–2007. *Hispanic-Latino Farmers and Ranchers Project: Final Report*. Gainesville: University of Florida Center for
Organic Agriculture, Department of Family, Youth, and Community Sciences.
Accessed February 2, 2019. https://nifa.usda.gov/sites/default/files/asset/document/
hispanic_full_report.pdf.

Teubal, Miguel. 2009. "Agrarian Reform and Social Movements in the Age of Globalization: Latin America at the Dawn of the Twenty-First Century." Translated by
Mariana Ortega Breña. *Latin American Perspectives* 36 (4): 9–20.

Trauger, Amy. 2017. *We Want Land to Live: Making Political Space for Food Sovereignty*.
Geographies of Justice and Social Transformation Series Book 33. Athens: University
of Georgia Press.

Tucker, Davis, and Jessi Creller. 2007. 1917 Immigration Act. University of Washington at Bothell. Accessed June 12, 2017. http://library.uwb.edu/Static/USimmigration/
1917_immigration_act.html.

Urdanivia, Claudia. 2018. "Food Sovereignty and Farmers of Color: An Interview
with Natasha Bowens." *Food Tank*. Accessed June 19, 2018. https://foodtank.com/
news/2015/08/food-sovereignty-and-farmers-of-color-an-interview-with-natasha
-bowens/.

USDA (US Department of Agriculture). 2014. Census of Agriculture. Accessed
November 2, 2015. www.agcensus.usda.gov.

USDA-ERS (US Department of Agriculture, Economic Research Service). 2017. *Glossary*. Accessed October 25, 2018. https://www.ers.usda.gov/topics/farm-economy/
farm-household-well-being/glossary/.

USDA-ERS (US Department of Agriculture, Economic Research Service). 2018.
Organic Trade. Last modified January 19, 2018. https://www.ers.usda.gov/topics/
natural-resources-environment/organic-agriculture/organic-trade.

USDA-OASCR (US Department of Agriculture, Office of the Assistant Secretary
for Civil Rights). 2015. *Secretary Vilsack's Efforts to Address Discrimination at USDA*.
Accessed January 6, 2015. http://www.ascr.usda.gov/cr_at_usda.html.

US Department of State, Office of the Historian. 2017. The Immigration Act of 1924 (The Johnson-Reed Act). Accessed May 1, 2017. https://history.state.gov/milestones/1921-1936/immigration-act.

van der Ploeg, Jan Douwe. 2012. *The New Peasantries: Struggles for Autonomy and Sustainability in an Era of Empire and Globalization*. New York: Routledge.

van der Ploeg, Jan Douwe. 2013. *Peasants and the Art of Farming: A Chayanovian Manifesto*. Halifax: Fernwood Publishing.

van der Ploeg, Jan Douwe. 2014. "Peasant-Driven Agricultural Growth and Food Sovereignty." *Journal of Peasant Studies* 41, no. 6 (November): 999–1030.

Van Sant, Levi. 2016. "'Into the Hands of Negroes': Reproducing Plantation Geographies in the South Carolina Lowcountry." *Geoforum* 77 (December): 196–205.

Vázquez-Castillo, Maria Teresa. 2004. *Land Privatization in Mexico: Urbanization, Formation of Regions and Globalization in Ejidos*. New York: Routledge.

Vilsack, Thomas J. 2009. "A New Civil Rights Era for USDA." Memorandum. US Department of Agriculture, Department of the Secretary, Washington, DC. Accessed June 4, 2018. http://eeo21.com/memos_usda_new_civil_rights_era_4_09.html.

Walker, Richard. 2004. *The Conquest of Bread: 150 Years of Agribusiness in California*. New York: New Press.

Wells, Miriam J. 1984. "The Resurgence of Sharecropping: Historical Anomaly or Political Strategy?" *American Journal of Sociology* 90, no. 2 (July): 1–29.

Wells, Miriam J. 1991. "Ethnic Groups and Knowledge Systems in Agriculture." *Economic Development and Cultural Change* 39, no. 4 (July): 739–771.

Wells, Miriam J. 1996. *Strawberry Fields: Politics, Class, and Work in California Agriculture*. Ithaca, NY: Cornell University Press.

Welsh, Rick. 1997. "Vertical Coordination, Producer Response, and the Locus of Control over Agricultural Production Decisions." *Rural Sociology* 62, no. 4 (December): 491–507.

Welsh, Rick, and Leland Glenna. 2006. "Considering the Role of the University in Conducting Research on Agri-Biotechnologies." *Social Studies of Science* 36, no. 6 (December): 929–942.

Williams-Forson, Psyche A. 2006. *Building Houses out of Chicken Legs: Black Women, Food, and Power*. Chapel Hill: University of North Carolina Press.

Williamson, Joel. 1965. *After Slavery: The Negro in South Carolina during Reconstruction, 1861–1877*. Chapel Hill: University of North Carolina Press.

Wittman, Hannah, Annette Aurelie Desmarais, and Nettie Wiebe. 2010. "The Origins and Potential of Food Sovereignty." In *Food Sovereignty: Reconnecting Food, Nature and Community*, edited by Hannah Wittman, Annette Aurelie Desmarais, and Nettie Wiebe, 1–14. Halifax: Fernwood Publishing.

Zandt, Alyson. 2014. "Northern Neck, Virginia." In *State of the South: Building an Infrastructure of Opportunity for the Next Generation*. Durham, NC: MDC. http://stateofthesouth.org/wp-content/uploads/2014/11/MDC_StateOfTheSouth_web.pdf.

Zippert, John. 2015. "USDA Approves Only 14% of Completed Claims in the Hispanic and Women Farmers and Ranchers Discrimination Settlement." *Greene County Democrat*. Accessed November 15, 2015. http://greenecountydemocrat.com/?p=14384.

Index

United Farm Workers, 43–44
USDA (US Department of Agriculture),
11, 12, 13, 129–130, 165
census data and staff of, 9, 11, 22
Cooperative State Research, Education,
and Extension Service, 60
discrimination against black farmers
by, 58–59
funding programs for farmers, 53–57
Hispanic Farmers and Ranchers
discrimination suit and claims, 13
hoop house installation program
promoted by, 53
as institutional boundary for Latino/a
immigrant farmers, 97–98
lack of awareness about Latino/a
immigrant farmers, 10
lawsuits against and changes at, 63–
74, 169
National Agricultural Statistics Service
(NASS), 45–50
new funding to support socially
disadvantaged farmers, 98–101, 166
nonwhite staff at, 168
outreach staff at, 12, 61–62
overt racism at offices of, 35
paperwork and standardization with,
75–82, 85
regulation of "organic" term by, 7,
113
Spanish-language forms from, 62,
75–76
support for large-scale production of
commodity crops, 57
Sustainable Agriculture Research and
Education program, 60
undocumented farmers as ineligible
for programs through, 5

Van der Ploeg, Jan Douwe, 137
Van Sant, Levi, 51
Villa, Francisco "Pancho," 141
Vilsack, Thomas, 63, 97

Virginia's Northern Neck, farmers of,
17–18, 53, 61–62, 73–74, 83–84
Viva Farms, 20–21, 71, 161–162

Washington State, farmers of, 20–22,
71, 81, 91–92
Wells, Miriam, 58, 152
Whiteness, 29, 30, 51
World War I era and Mexican
immigrants, 38–40

YES! Magazine, 163

Zapata, Emilio, 141

Food, Health, and the Environment

Series Editor: Robert Gottlieb, Henry R. Luce Professor of Urban and Environmental Policy, Occidental College